D1521418

# Prison Food in America

Rowman & Littlefield Studies in Food and Gastronomy

**General Editor:** Ken Albala, Professor of History,
University of the Pacific (kalbala@pacific.edu)
**Rowman & Littlefield Executive Editor:**
Suzanne Staszak-Silva (sstaszak-silva@rowman.com)

Food studies is a vibrant and thriving field encompassing not only cooking and eating habits but also issues such as health, sustainability, food safety, and animal rights. Scholars in disciplines as diverse as history, anthropology, sociology, literature, and the arts focus on food. The mission of **Rowman & Littlefield Studies in Food and Gastronomy** is to publish the best in food scholarship, harnessing the energy, ideas, and creativity of a wide array of food writers today. This broad line of food-related titles will range from food history, interdisciplinary food studies monographs, general interest series, and popular trade titles to textbooks for students and budding chefs, scholarly cookbooks, and reference works.

*Appetites and Aspirations in Vietnam: Food and Drink in the Long Nineteenth Century*, by Erica J. Peters
*Three World Cuisines: Italian, Mexican, Chinese*, by Ken Albala
*Food and Social Media: You Are What You Tweet*, by Signe Rousseau
*Food and the Novel in Nineteenth-Century America*, by Mark McWilliams
*Man Bites Dog: Hot Dog Culture in America*, by Bruce Kraig and Patty Carroll
*A Year in Food and Beer: Recipes and Beer Pairings for Every Season*, by Emily Baime and Darin Michaels
*Celebraciones Mexicanas: History, Traditions, and Recipes*, by Andrea Lawson Gray and Adriana Almazán Lahl
*The Food Section: Newspaper Women and the Culinary Community*, by Kimberly Wilmot Voss
*Small Batch: Pickles, Cheese, Chocolate, Spirits, and the Return of Artisanal Foods*, by Suzanne Cope
*Food History Almanac: Over 1,300 Years of World Culinary History, Culture, and Social Influence*, by Janet Clarkson
*Cooking and Eating in Renaissance Italy: From Kitchen to Table*, by Katherine A. McIver
*Eating Together: Food, Space, and Identity in Malaysia and Singapore*, by Jean Duruz and Gaik Cheng Khoo

*Nazi Hunger Politics: A History of Food in the Third Reich*, by Gesine Gerhard
*The Carrot Purple and Other Curious Stories of the Food We Eat*, by Joel S. Denker
*Food in the Gilded Age: What Ordinary Americans Ate*, by Robert Dirks
*Urban Foodways and Communication: Ethnographic Studies in Intangible Cultural Food Heritages Around the World*, by Casey Man Kong Lum and Marc de Ferrière le Vayer
*Food, Health, and Culture in Latino Los Angeles*, by Sarah Portnoy
*Food Cults: How Fads, Dogma, and Doctrine Influence Diet*, by Kima Cargill
*Prison Food in America*, by Erika Camplin

# Prison Food in America

Erika Camplin

ROWMAN & LITTLEFIELD
*Lanham • Boulder • New York • London*

Published by Rowman & Littlefield
A wholly owned subsidary of The Rowman & Littlefield Publishing Group, Inc.
4501 Forbes Boulevard, Suite 200, Lanham, Maryland 20706
www.rowman.com

Unit A, Whitacre Mews, 26-34 Stannary Street, London SE11 4AB

British Library Cataloguing in Publication Information Available

**Library of Congress Cataloging-in-Publication Data**
Names: Camplin, Erika, author.
Title: Prison food in America / Erika Camplin.
Description: Lanham : Rowman & Littlefield, [2016] | Series: Rowman & Littlefield studies in food and gastronomy | Includes bibliographical references and index.
Identifiers: LCCN 2016028436 (print) | LCCN 2016043821 (ebook) | ISBN 9781442253476 (cloth : alk. paper) | ISBN 9781442253483 (Electronic)
Subjects: LCSH: Prisons—Food service—United States—History. | Prisoners—Nutrition—United States—History. | Food habits—United States—History.
Classification: LCC HV8847 .C36 2016 (print) | LCC HV8847 (ebook) | DDC 365/.66—dc23
LC record available at https://lccn.loc.gov/2016028436

∞™ The paper used in this publication meets the minimum requirements of American National Standard for Information Sciences—Permanence of Paper for Printed Library Materials, ANSI/NISO Z39.48-1992.

Printed in the United States of America

# Contents

# 1

# America's Prison System
# and the Role of Food in It

A n entire book about prison food would be remiss if it did not discuss a general
overview of the United States' current prison population and how we came to
a point in history, which many consider an epidemic of incarceration. The population of people currently "locked up" or "behind bars" in the United States has skyrocketed in the last three decades to a total number of around 2 million inmates at
any given time: That number is composed of the approximately 100,000 in federal
custody, 1.1 million in state custody, and 600,000 in local jails.[1] Quite simply put,
nobody in the world incarcerates more people than the United States. As a country,
we have less than 5 percent of the world's population and almost 25 percent of its
incarcerated population.[2] One in thirty-five adults are under some form of correctional control (counting prison, jail, parole, and probation populations). As will be
discussed, a number of historical situations and political decisions led to a massive
expansion of the federal prison system over the past forty years: an increase of almost 500 percent.[3] The point of attempting to wrap our minds around this immense
population, within the context of this book, is to consider the number of mouths
being fed in this system. Food is a huge part of the equation that defines our prison
system, if for no other reason than volume: We feed the incarcerated over 13 billion
meals each year. So, what are we feeding prisoners? Who is feeding them? How
does this play into their welfare and a notion of rehabilitation? Does it?

❖ ❖ ❖

America's general fascination with prison life and the culture that surrounds it has always existed, but has been rising over the past decade or so, thanks in part to Hollywood's portrayal of life behind bars through such shows as *Oz*, *Orange Is the New Black*, *Breakout Kings*, and *Prison Break*, to name just a few. A number of documentary-style television shows on channels such as A&E (*Scared Straight, Behind Bars: Rookie Year, 60 Days In*) showcase what life is like for inmates, correctional officers, or women in prison. In addition, celebrity run-ins with the law seem not-so-uncommon these days, and scores of people flock to the Internet to gawk at mug shots and read about how the people they have watched in movies or on television are faring behind bars. Whether it's Martha Stewart's insider trading sentence or Lindsay Lohan's bi-annual DUI that sends her to county lock-up, we as a population are often fascinated with what the day-to-day is like for them.

However, when it comes to facing the true realities of our penal system, we often love to gawk at the sensationalized version and then cower to face what is actually happening. A common notion in the comments on the many articles about prison food scattered across the Internet reveals a decidedly simple refrain: If you don't want to eat prison food, don't go to prison. Many people said such things as "cry me a river!" "Am I supposed to feel bad for what the criminals and rapists eat?" and, "Many people in our country don't even get to eat this good!" Unfortunately, however, this is an oversimplification for many reasons, such as the fact that we as a nation incarcerate an incredible number of nonviolent offenders as well as innocent people. It also fails to take into account the fact that if we aim to make productive and contributory citizens out of former criminals (who will inevitably reenter society most of the time), then we should consider all aspects of their rehabilitation, including the vitalness of food.

Therein lies an interesting type of duality that exists in the American consciousness: On the one hand, we love the salacious prison story told to us by Hollywood. On the other, we do not want to see or hear anything about real prisons, or to think deeply about their consequences, and we prefer to literally and figuratively marginalize that population of our country to the periphery.

## PRISON BY THE NUMBERS

America has, both by sheer numbers and per capita, the most incarcerated people of any developed nation in the world. That is an overwhelming and staggering statistic for a country that prides itself on allowing equal opportunity for all citizens to live the "American Dream," which holds that all citizens are given the same tools for success and that they can succeed with hard work. This vision, albeit a nice story, is an incredible fallacy when we consider the number of people that we have pushed to the margins in this society, left with very few chances and opportunities, gone and forgotten behind bars in a system of "corrections" that seems broken and ineffective (the recidivism, a return to prison after release, rate hovers around 60 percent on average[4]).

On the whole, there are around 2 million incarcerated people in America on any given day. According to the Bureau of Justice, at year end of 2014, 612 people per 100,000 residents age eighteen or older were imprisoned.[5] That is about one in one hundred adults. Our reputation for incarceration is global: According to what is considered the go-to global source on prison statistics worldwide, the *World Prison Brief*, the United States has about 4.4 percent of the world's population within its borders, but over 22 percent of the world's total prison population.[6] That is to say that 22 percent of all the people incarcerated in the world are in the United States. If that is not staggering enough, consider that we currently have more people imprisoned than occupy the cities of Atlanta, Minneapolis, Miami, and New Orleans combined. If one takes into account all of the people under "supervision of the adult correctional system" in the United States—that is everyone in prisons and jails, as well as those on parole, in detention centers, and such—this would total an estimated 6,899,000 persons according to the Bureau of Justice Statistics.[7] Taking that into account, this total population, if brought together, would form the second largest city in the United States.

What this means for a book about prison food in particular is quite simply that we as a nation are effectively feeding around 2 million mouths at least three times over each and every day. That is an estimated 6 million meals per day, which comes to a yearly total of, at minimum, 13.14 billion meals served. Correctional facility operators could indeed justify borrowing the McDonald's slogan of "Billions and Billions Served," since it is rightly the case each year.

Thankfully, we have begun to see a glimpse at a new direction, as the country has begun to see that a large prison population has drained resources and strained communities. The movement toward reform of our criminal justice system is a long time coming, but one that seems to bridge the divide between political parties. As Maurice Chamah reported on *The Marshall Project*, "In February 2015, the American Civil Liberties Union (ACLU), the Center for American Progress, FreedomWorks, and Koch Industries (three politically divergent entities) announced they would collaborate to back the Coalition for Public Safety and lobby to reduce mandatory-minimum sentences, support alternatives to incarceration, and reduce the overall prison population."[8] What this indicates is a direction of reform and change after years of heading in the wrong direction.

## RAPID GROWTH OF PRISON POPULATION 1980–PRESENT

Since the 1980s, policy changes in criminal justice, among other factors, have resulted in this incredible jump in the incarcerated population of the United States. Since that time, the prison population has more than tripled from 307,276 prisoners in 1978 to over 1.6 million in 2009.[9] A very slight decline was seen in the subsequent three years. A vital fact about this increase is the effect it has had on African American men, who are incarcerated at an disproportionate rate to any other population—more on that shortly.

The number of people incarcerated for drug crimes (often nonviolent) has been the most-cited and most likely culprit for the extensive increase in our country's prison epidemic. There are more people behind bars today for drug offenses than there were in the entire prison population in 1980.[10] The War on Drugs, started by President Richard Nixon in 1971, and catalyzed through the 1980s by the administrations of Presidents Ronald Reagan and George H. W. Bush, was an attempt to take down "public enemy number one" (aka drugs) that has progressed from an endeavor to reclaim neighborhoods and safety to wedging an incredible schism between populations by incarcerating incredible numbers of people, mainly young black men. Longer sentencing laws and tougher crackdowns on nonviolent drug offenses began to make the prison population swell. Only very recently have federal officials such as President Barack Obama begun to commute the sentences of some nonviolent drug offenders under criminal justice law reforms. As the social justice advocate and University of Pennsylvania Law School professor Dorothy E. Roberts points out:

> The War on Drugs is responsible for [the] level of black incarceration. The explosion of both the prison population and its racial disparity are largely attributable to aggressive street-level enforcement of the drug laws and harsh sentencing of drug offenders. An increasingly large proportion of new admissions for drug offenses combined with longer mandatory sentences to keep prison populations at historically high levels during the 1990s, despite declines in crime. The War on Drugs became its own prisoner-generating machine.[11]

This, in turn, became an epidemic in the country of continually locking up nonviolent offenders for drug-related crimes, and thus overstuffing and overcrowding our prisons, leading to the expansion in the population of prisoners and the number of prisons.

In addition to the increase in incarceration rates for nonviolent offenses, sentences have increased over the years. According to the Sentencing Project:

> Harsh sentencing laws like mandatory minimums, combined with cutbacks in parole release, keep people in prison for longer periods of time. The National Research Council reported that half of the 222 percent growth in the state prison population between 1980 and 2010 was due to an increase of time served in prison for all offenses. There has also been a historic rise in the use of life sentences: one in nine people in prison is now serving a life sentence, nearly a third of whom are sentenced to life without parole.[12]

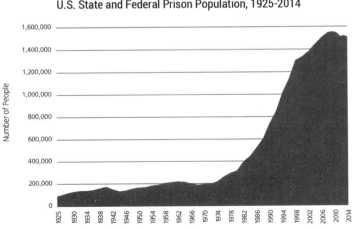

**U.S. State and Federal Prison Population, 1925-2014**

Source: Bureau of Justice Statistics *Prisoners Series.*

## THE PRISON-INDUSTRIAL COMPLEX

With the expansion of the prison system due to the large influx of population came the opportunity for companies to capitalize in a newly expanded industry by providing goods and services to facilities that the state and federal governments could not handle on their own anymore. This has led to the creation of what some people term a "prison-industrial complex" (a term first coined by the journalist and author Eric Schlosser in his 1998 exposé article on the topic of the same name). The term describes a state in which, despite the fact that violent crime has declined, the prison population continues to grow and along with it the pocketbooks of those servicing US corrections facilities. This is, according to Schlosser's *Atlantic* article:

> a set of bureaucratic, political, and economic interests that encourage increased spending on imprisonment, regardless of the actual need. The prison-industrial complex is not a conspiracy, guiding the nation's criminal-justice policy behind closed doors. It is a confluence of special interests that has given prison construction in the United States a seemingly unstoppable momentum.[13]

Foodservice is one of the major service offerings that have, generally, been outsourced to corporations. As Schlosser says, "As the prison industry has grown, it has assumed many of the attributes long associated with the defense industry. The line between the public interest and private interests has blurred."[14] The prison-industrial complex is so elaborate that entire trade shows, conferences, and magazines are dedicated to the latest news on how best to run services while simultaneously cutting costs and maximizing the bottom line. Food, being one of the largest expenses in running a correctional facility, lies at the heart of this matter.

## RACE AND INCARCERATION

The overall statistics of incarceration and corrections are mind-blowing on their own, but turn even bleaker when we look at the specific demographics of who is incarcerated. In 2014, African American men had the highest imprisonment rate in every age group and were in state or federal facilities 3.8 to 10.5 times more often than white men and 1.4 to 3.1 times more often than Hispanic men.[15] What that means is that, in this country, blacks are incarcerated seven times as often as whites.

While recognizing the vastness of the topic of race and incarceration and the amount of important work having been done on the issue, this book is by no means going to scratch the surface on such a vital and complicated topic. However, it is necessary to dedicate a brief moment to the issue, in part because of how often it surfaces in research, but also because it is completely tied up with food. On the whole, it is decidedly impossible and inappropriate to write anything about the American incarceration issue without recognizing the disproportionate rate at which we lock up African Americans when compared to their white counterparts. As the ACLU Web site states:

> The War on Drugs has been a war on communities of color. The racial disparities are staggering: Despite the fact that white and black people use drugs at similar rates, black people are jailed on drug charges ten times more often than white people are. Black people are also three times more likely to be arrested for marijuana than white people are.[16]

According to the Drug Policy Alliance:

> Black people comprise 13 percent of the US population, and are consistently documented by the US government to use drugs at similar rates to people of other races. But black people comprise 30 percent of those arrested for drug law violations—and nearly 40 percent of those incarcerated in state or federal prison for drug law violations.[17]

Incarceration and its consequences are much more of a reality and part of life for black communities than they are for others. In an article called "The Caging of America: Why Do We Lock Up so Many People?" published in *The New Yorker* in 2012, author Adam Gopnik calls the United States out on its abominable incarceration practices, stating that, "The scale and brutality of our prisons are the moral scandal of American life."[18] He continues, "For a great many poor people in America, particularly poor black men, prison is a destination that braids through an ordinary life, much as high school and college do for rich white ones. More than half of black men without a high school diploma go to prison in their lives."[19] Many social justice advocates have begun to recognize that for hundreds of thousands of young black American males, their destiny seems decided for them: "Young black men pass quickly from a period of police harassment into a period of 'formal control' (i.e., actual imprisonment) and then are doomed for life into a system of 'invisible control.' Prevented from voting, legally discriminated against for the rest of their lives, most will cycle back through the prison system."[20]

Serving the sentence imposed by the state does not mean that one is then free of the label "criminal" as the system would lead one to believe. Michelle Alexander summarizes the current carceral state in her brilliant book breaking down the system and cycle of mass incarceration entitled *The New Jim Crow: Mass Incarceration in the Age of Colorblindness*:

Today it is perfectly legal to discriminate against criminals in nearly all the ways that it was once legal to discriminate against African Americans. If you are labeled a felon, old forms of discrimination—employment, discrimination, housing discrimination, denial of the right to vote, denial of educational opportunity, denial of food stamps and other public benefits, and exclusions from jury service—are suddenly legal. As a criminal, you have scarcely more rights, and arguably less respect, than a black man living in Alabama at the height of Jim Crow.[21]

It begs the question as to whether we as a society have reverted to the days of Jim Crow or simply continued this mass discrimination in a new form and brought it into the current era. It is important to note how deeply pervasive this problem is: Research has shown evidence that prosecutors are twice as likely to pursue a mandatory minimum sentence for black people as for whites charged with precisely the same offense."[22]

## FOOD, RACE, AND PRISON

As noted above, we as a nation feed millions and millions of mouths in prisons and jails across this country every single day. It has also been pointed out that a large portion of those being fed are African American males, and it seems worthwhile to point out the landscapes from which they grew up, specifically their food landscapes.

In an era when America is reconsidering what the Civil Rights Movement accomplished, we are finding that, despite the incredible work of that time period, systemic racism pervades in a manner perhaps just as rampant as ever before. It is simply more hidden from plain sight. A large component of this issue is poverty and a large component of poverty is food. With the emergence of the Black Lives Matter movement and amid the deaths of many young black men at the hands of white police officers, criminal justice and its practices are highly contentious topics. And, as the food journalist Kristin Wartman pointed out in her article of the same title, "food belongs in our discussions of race."[23]

Why? As Wartman clarifies:

Just as our economy has become starkly stratified with wealth concentrated at the top, it is increasingly clear that we live in a two-tiered food system in which the wealthy tend to eat well and are rewarded with better health, while the poor tend to eat low-quality diets, causing their health to suffer. A report released last year by the Harvard School of Public Health found that while diet quality improved among people of high socioeconomic status, it deteriorated among those at the other end of the spectrum, and the gap doubled between 2000 and 2010.[24]

Many of the young people that end up in prison grew up hungry or in food deserts. And, according to Roberts, "Research in several cities reveals that the exit and re-entry of inmates is geographically concentrated in the poorest, minority neighborhoods. As many as 1 in 8 of the adult male residents of these urban areas is sent to prison each year and 1 in 4 is behind bars on any given day."[25]

More generally, food, race, and prison are all linked, because our identities are entirely tied up with what we eat. As sociologist Rebecca Godderis purports, "the foods we eat and the circumstances under which we consume, extend beyond our biological need for fuel. They are also based on an individual's cultural, political, and familial heritage. Thus, the symbolic importance of food and consumptive rituals arises from the fact that these choices are representative of our individual and collective identities."[26] In prison, the meaning of food is rich and tied up with politics—both on the inside and outside of the prison walls.

All this is to say that it seems to correlate that the same populations living in poverty and food deserts are often those becoming incarcerated. In something that has been dubbed the "School to Prison Pipeline" by the ACLU and others, it is not uncommon for a young person to spend the first eighteen years of his or her life under the guidance of a heavily disciplinary "zero tolerance" education system, fail out, and fall into the hands of the juvenile discipline system, followed by prison. Not surprisingly, those most likely to be on this pipeline are African American and Hispanic children, mostly male. Those with a history of abuse and neglect are also stuck in this trajectory more frequently.[27] One common denominator in being institutionalized for such a lengthy period is food. Not only are the choices of this population appropriated by the institution, but so are, quite literally, their stomachs and their diets. Therefore, the takeover is mental, physical, and physiological. And, as will be discussed later, many of the same companies feeding our children in schools are feeding prisoners. It is not unfathomable at all that someone growing up in a rough neighborhood eats mostly institutional food his or her entire life. That is a particularly overwhelming thought to someone that studies food and its implications for health, culture, and society.

Compounding these statistics is the fact that, again, incarceration rates have tripled since 1980.

It is also worth noting that, in this same time period (since 1980), the rates of diet-related diseases such as heart disease, diabetes, and cancer skyrocketed, especially among minority populations, as the nation moved from what nutritionist and food scholar Marion Nestle has termed an "eat more" ethos to an "eat less" one in government, but not for big food corporations who maintained the strong marketing of unhealthy foods.[28] Nestle notes on her blog *Food Politics*:

For decades, rates of overweight and obesity in the United States stayed about the same. But in the early 1980s, rates increased sharply and continued to increase through the 1990s. . . . The increases [of obesity and overweight people] correlated closely with deregulatory policies that encouraged greater farm production and loosened restrictions on food marketing. These led to an increase in the number of calories available in the food supply.[29]

Bringing this all together, the 1980s become an intensely significant point for the purposes of our understanding of what one could consider the degradation of our prison system *and* our food system in America: We see at that time period a sharp increase in the rates of diet-related disease, the number of incarcerated people, and the gap between the wealthy and the poor. This trifecta has proven hugely problematic to our society's well-being.

## DIET AND INCARCERATION

Entrance into the system of corrections so often already from the societal periphery (poverty, poor neighborhoods, lack of education) is the end of lifestyle normalcy, and diets and mealtime play a large role in this normalcy. Prison is the removal of the self from daily life, both from the physical and temporal world, but also the removal of the known self from those sources of daily routine that anchor a human life. What is life without one's own time, place, and pleasures?

While the notion of time as you know it on the outside is taken away, in prison time becomes centered on food. Mealtimes and food are a clock, a series of anchor points throughout each day, and a milestone for each passage against a backdrop of nothingness: What orders the day is a strict regimen of intermittent mastication on mediocre meals. Food takes on many, many facets: It is what paces the day, it is one of the few reminders of "the outside" and family, it is the foundation of an economy within the prison walls, and it is, as one inmate told me, the number one topic of conversation. He told me people would talk about food extensively, unendingly to each other every single day: "What's for lunch?" "That chili was some cold trash!" and when people come back from a visit with family in the visitation room, the first thing they would ask them is what they got from the vending machines.[30]

Food is psychological, physiological, and social, and that is why it is and can be a powerful, transformative tool. The effects of diet on inmates have been studied by scientists attempting to decode biocriminology and how environmental factors play a role in the behaviors of criminals and inmates. Poor diets can lead to all sorts of behavioral and mood issues. In an extensive 1988 study titled "The Effects of Diet on Behavior: Implications for Criminology and Corrections," Dr. Diana Fishbein and Dr. Susan Pease outlined the potentially profound effects that diet can have in relation to inmate behavior by compiling scientific evidence surrounding food allergies, hypoglycemia, trace elements (toxins), and food dyes and additives. Hypoglycemia (low blood sugar due to lack of food or eating highly refined carbs) alone can lead to a host of symptoms, including

> fatigue, irritability, nervousness, depression, vertigo, faintness, insomnia, mental confusion, inability to concentrate, anxiety, phobias, dysperceptions, destructive outbursts, headaches, heart palpitations, muscle cramps, convulsions, digestive disturbances, allergies, blurred vision, lack of sex drive in women, impotence in men, and difficulty in performing simple physical or mental tasks.[31]

Imagine having any one of those symptoms—would you act like your normal "self"? What's more is that a number of other studies point to better behavior when diets are rich in, or supplemented by, vitamins or other nutrients. People have been linking diet and behavior for years and many recently have bridged the connection between the behavior of schoolchildren and what we are feeding them, with a big push toward healthier school meals to improve academic performance, increase attention spans, and reduce sick days.[32] These principles can and should also be applied to populations such as prisons and the correctional system, where the link between diet and rehabilitation or even just general behavior seems to be less and less of a factor in meal planning. One study that examined the effects of Omega-3 fatty acids on 231 young adult prisoners concluded that "Antisocial behaviour in prisons, including violence, are reduced by vitamins, minerals and essential fatty acids with similar implications for those eating poor diets in the community."[33]

In addition, food is emotional and has proven time and time again to be a connector and a divider. This is no truer than for the incarcerated, whose choices and freedoms around food have been mostly revoked. As Bryan Finoki said online at *GOOD Magazine*, "food takes on a precarious new set of meanings and moral functionality [in prison]. Food more or less becomes a biopolitical digestive tract through which power is contested and transmitted, both as a weapon in the disciplinary tactics of the jailer, and as a currency on the black market within prison culture."[34]

## WHAT ABOUT REHABILITATION?

We call our system the Department of Corrections, or simply Corrections, but correcting or any notion of rehabilitation has been largely thrown to the wayside in favor of punitive action through the revocation of selfhood. "Corrections" now refers to placing people in an ironic state of having nothing but time, and no freedom to choose what to do with it. Imagine a yearlong or lifelong waiting room or plane ride. Imagine the confinement and constraint of those situations, but add incessant noise, aggravated energies, no privacy (even to go to the bathroom), and little to no corner of escape: "Prison, with its daily rhythm, with the transfer and the defense, does not leave any time; prison dissolves time: This is the principal form of punishment in a capitalist society," said Italian philosopher Antonio Negri after spending time incarcerated.[35] America sends its criminals to unseen corners of our society, where they live monotonous lives that take away autonomy and choice, and where their time is completely owned by the institution. Perhaps due to the sheer volume of prison populations, institutions of incarceration seem to simply be trying to get by on the absolute least they can put in, checking the minimum of boxes, and spending more time dealing with gangs, overcrowding, and the incredible difficulty of controlling a population of this magnitude, rather than thinking through how to rehabilitate them or get them back on their feet again.

As it is important to know how we got here, this book will examine prison food in its current state, how it shapes the day-to-day operations of correctional facilities, and just what and how we are feeding this massive portion of the population.

# 2

# A Brief History of Prison Food

Early in the spring the whole of the inmates broke out in open mutiny. Their alleged grievance was the issue of an inferior kind of bread. Change of dietary scales in prisons is always attended with some risk of disturbance, even when discipline is most rigorously maintained. In those early days of mild government riot was of course inevitable. The committee having thought fit to alter the character of the flour supplied, soon afterwards, at breakfast-time, all the prisoners, male and female, refused to receive their bread. . . . Next day, Sunday, the bread was at first taken, then all alike, in spite of exhortations of their visitor, Mr. Holford, left it outside their cell doors. Next day, Sunday, the bread was at first taken, then thrown out into the passages. The governor determined to have Divine Service as usual, but to provide against what might happen, deposited within his pew "three brace of pistols loaded with ball." To make matters worse, the Chancellor of the Exchequer arrived with a party of friends to attend the service. The governor immediately pointed out that he was apprehensive that "in consequence of the newly adopted bread the prisoners' conduct would not be orderly, as it had ordinarily been." At first the male prisoners were satisfied by raising and letting fall the flaps of the kneeling benches with a loud report, and throwing loaves about in the body of the chapel, while the women in an audible tone cried out, "Give us our daily bread."

—Account of a riot at Millbank Prison in England
from *Memorials of Millbank*, written in 1875 by Arthur Griffiths[1]

There is no one clearly outlined history of prison food, as this chapter may imply, but to understand the current paradigm of prison food, it proves interesting to dig into what can be found in the past. Much of the way food has been shaped and formed in prisons is due to the cultural thought about prisoners in general, and how they should be treated by society and by the state. Food in prison is a reflection of culture and cultural thinking about criminal justice and reform. And like much of American history, the history of our prison system—its formation and thought surrounding it—is linked very tightly to England. In that regard, and because digging a bit deeper into the past is so fascinating, we will focus a good portion of the chapter on English prison history, its use and conception of food, and how it came to influence the American prison system. It should be noted that the term "prison" is used somewhat loosely in the above and below descriptors. It is not truly until the middle of the nineteenth century that America has a real prison in the sense that we understand it today. Punishment for crimes did not turn into prison sentences, but usually went two ways: (1) The offender paid a debt proportionate to their crime, or (2) they ended up in a "workhouse" doing manual labor. In fact, as the twentieth-century scholar on the topic Harry Elmer Barnes notes, "at the beginning of the eighteenth century imprisonment was unusual, except as applied to political and religious offenders and debtors, while before the middle of the nineteenth century it was the conventional method of punishing crime in both Europe and America."[2] A true prison *system* is an even more modern creation.

## ENGLAND'S PRISON HISTORY

If you pore long enough over records and accounts of prisons in English history, you come to find that the marginalized and societally sidelined beings, the prisoners, in telling their stories, really say much more about their fellow countrymen in their accounts than about themselves. The implications of a greater societal ideology and notions of zeitgeist shine through when one looks at the lives and details of the people on the periphery.

The question we will delve into in this chapter—which is centered on the history of prison food in England and America—asks if there were any connection between food and rehabilitation in the planning and execution of prison dietaries, past and present. In reading this history of prisons, it seems to be a reoccurring age-old question: When should food be a mode of punishment and when should it be nutritious and physically satiating in an effort to rehabilitate? Within a chronological framework, we will examine notions of rehabilitation in English prison history dietaries and end up with only more questions of why and how any connection between diet and rehabilitation is generally not considered. We will move (generally) from medieval times to the eighteenth then nineteenth centuries and land close to the present day.

## MEDIEVAL PRISON DIETS

Prisons seemed to be a major fixture of the Middle Ages. This was especially true for those unable to pay their debts to the given monarchy of the day, as it was common practice for a person living in the Middle Ages to be sent to prison for simply being too poor. The sparsest knowledge of prison diets comes from this time period, as real prison records were not kept until the late seventeenth century, so information is derived from individual testimony and government and law records that often only allude to prison conditions.[3] What is known about food in these prisons is even scarcer, but what emerges is that there was a distinct hierarchy within the prison walls, just as outside of them, based on economic wealth and class status, and food was a large part of this structure.

Fleet Prison and Newgate Prison, both located near the city of London, offer us some accounts of the food situation prisoners experienced during medieval times. Newgate was the prison for hard criminals of the time, housing those that had committed more horrific or appalling crimes. The circumstances these inmates were exposed to certainly reflected a viler version of punishment—dungeon-like cells for many of the prisons, conditions ripe for the ever-feared "gaol fever." "Gaol," the colloquial term for prison, and the fever being generally either scurvy or typhus, which was constantly running rampant and ravaging the lives of many prisoners at the time.[4] Newgate suffered from many riots, attempts at mutiny, and general brutality. Fleet Prison was reserved for committers of lesser offenses, and "The majority of prisoners were held either for debt or fine."[5] Though not ideal, the conditions at Fleet seemed slightly paramount to those at Newgate, especially before a much-needed makeover at Newgate in the late 1400s. Of most interest to our topic is the fact that this overhaul of the current structure yielded as the "main feature of the new prison . . . a central hall where meals could be served, and which had the added convenience of a drinking fountain."[6]

Despite the implementation of a "modern"-style cafeteria at Newgate, what bubbles up in readings about both prisons is the fact that room, and especially board, were a far cry from a guarantee. Unlike what we are accustomed to understanding about the standard offering of three-squares in prison today, living, sleeping, and eating in Newgate and Fleet were costly (a special irony given that many prisoners were incarcerated for being too far in debt, unable to pay their dues to the city). Inmates were forced to pay a number of fees to get *into* the prison, *stay* in the prison, and *eat* in the prison. If they wanted any additional privileges (such as visitors or a trip to town), this was a further cost to be paid directly to the warden.[7]

The warden appears to have been the head of this small food economy within each prison's walls. That is to say, for a time the wardens were allowed to sell food, charcoal, candles, and other goods.[8] According to R. B. Pugh, author of a definitive text on the topic entitled *Imprisonment in Medieval England*, "there is indeed much evidence that prison-keepers tried to create a monopoly by making the importation of food difficult." And, perhaps most interestingly, "There is evidence, too, of the segregation of prisoners in messes, distinguished from one another by the social standing or wealth of prisoners."[9] In English prisons during medieval times, food was not a given, unlike in some of the contemporary prisons of the time in France and Italy.[10] Prisoners often relied on the charity of strangers or their relatives to simply allow them enough for bread and water while incarcerated.

A prevalent occurrence, as one can probably imagine, was starvation of prisoners. Those that could not afford food often literally starved to death in these mega-prisons in England. A somewhat common practice was for people to leave in their will their remaining funds as charity to the prisoners of one of their local prisons.[11] Some of the incarcerated, more rarely, found employment within the prison and even fewer were allowed to go to the city and beg during the day so that they could eke by. Those criminals with funds, on the other hand, "could live comfortably in the Fleet."[12] Unfortunately, not much more is known beyond bread, beer, wine, and water as part of the prison diet in medieval England (it seems that there was likely little else). The question of access to food *at all* becomes the most relevant piece at which to look in medieval times, insofar as I argue that having any food at all created a class-based economy within the prison walls. As in life, so it was in prison: those that could not afford to eat simply did not. Prison was no refuge from famine and debt—it was simply a microcosm of the real world hierarchy within a more confined space, with even less opportunity. Food (or lack thereof) was part of punishment, certainly, but interestingly, even the cruelest of offenders could eat and drink pretty well if they had the funds.


## REFORM: THE EIGHTEENTH CENTURY

Prison numbers soared in the seventeenth century when the practice of sending debtors to prison became even more common.[13] Overcrowding was a major issue and conditions, rather than improving, became even more dire. The onslaught of the Industrial Revolution meant the production of more things—more things for people to steal and be arrested on charges of petty crime for. At this point, bread and water were both rationed by municipal authorities, but regulation was scarce and "prison visits" (attempts by local and state governments to check up on the state of prisons) were even rarer. Any sort of nationally universal standards for prison diet remained to be developed. Additionally, "It was generally believed by both the public and the authorities that a restricted diet should form part of the discipline of punishment," and, as before, "starvation was often the fate of the poor."[14] Changes were needed, but only a few recognized such a need. We see in 1785, for example, the creation of Jeremy Bentham's notorious "panopticon" prison design, which was to be utilized for more optimal prisoner supervision.[15] But probably the widest-known prison reformer (in fact, really, the original prison reformer) was John Howard.

Inspired by his father, a strict Calvinist, Howard was a politician who began his career in prison reform as the High Sheriff of Bedfordshire, during which time he inspected the local prison and found the conditions abominable.[16] This sparked the desire for Howard to take on examining and overhauling the prison system in England. In his famous tome entitled *The State of Prison Systems in England and Wales*, originally published in 1777, Howard outlined in detail the haggard practices and downright inhumane conditions of prisons of the era.

Striking in his analysis is the centrality of diet to reform—reform for the prison, but also for the prisoner. Food is literally in the second paragraph of the book:

> There are several *bridewells* (to begin with them) in which prisoners have no allowance of Food at all. In some, the keeper farms what little is allowed them: and where he engages to supply each prisoner with one or two pennyworth of bread a day, I have known this shrunk to half, sometimes less than half the quantity, cut or broken from his own loaf.[17]

The entire text is peppered with an emphasis on the need for access to free medicine, bedding, and, above all, food (and in fact, *better* food on Sundays). Meat, however, was generally recommended to be excluded from prison diets, with the exception of maybe a Sunday dinner. Howard states:

> Here, as in the tap, I must insist upon it as highly necessary, that every gaoler, bridewell keeper, turnkey, etc. be excluded from all concern in the prisoners allowance; from all profit arising *directly* or *indirectly* from the sale of bread, or other food. Whoever distributes it should be free from all temptation to fraud: and be subject to a strong check. Scales and weights should be in all prisons, that the prisoners may see that they have their allowance.[18]

Howard's ideas of a Protestant work ethic seem to shine through here—he saw the prisoners in the gaols as coming out of prison (if they even made it out at all) being unfit for work, diseased, and broken down. His hope was to give them some societal worth; and diet, for him, was intricately linked to this notion.

Food was more than sustenance to Howard. In fact, one of his central reform ideas was *proper* diet:

> I have before said, that I am no advocate for luxury in the prisons; for I would have no meat diet for criminals in houses of correction, or at most, only on Sundays. Yet I would plead, that they should have a pound and a half of good household bread a day, and a quart of good beer: besides twice a day a quart of warm soup made from peas, rice, milk or barley. For a change they might sometimes have turnips, carrots or potatoes.[19]

Howard seems to understand the connection between health and food. He seems to understand that equality and food can help eliminate major power systems within the prison social structure and, as will be discussed later, he recognized the necessity to compensate for diet changes during times of illness. This is not to say that Howard was by any means the father of prison rehabilitation, but, instead of seeing inmates as societal refuse, he regarded them as having the potential to contribute to the greater social good in the future. This was an important step forward.

## AMERICANS AND PRISON REFORM IN THE EIGHTEENTH CENTURY

Americans were incredibly moved by Howard and his efforts abroad. As with much thinking of the time, papers, scholarly writings, and books were often brought back to the colonies from those that had recently been traveling in England and Europe. With Enlightenment thinking taking full hold there, much of this ideology found its way to America, particularly through influential people like Benjamin Franklin, who, having lived for a time in France, "was well acquainted with radical French thought."[20] Barnes's essay about the origin of America's penal system notes, "No other foreign philosopher so influenced the American Constitutional Convention of 1787 as did Montesquieu, and his exponents must have been nearly as familiar with his doctrines on the reform of criminal jurisprudence as with his theory of the separation of governmental powers."[21] These doctrines were entrenched in Enlightenment ideas about man's purpose: Very simply put, they believed that every man had a destiny, a purpose, and could be reformed through hard work and self-reflection. Franklin and a group of other strongly opinionated colonists began to ponder the topic of criminal justice and the treatment of criminals in America. They started a group aimed at reforming the current treatment of inmates called the Society for Alleviating the Miseries of Public Prisons. Their efforts brought sweeping reforms to crime laws and the creation of state prisons based in the notions of hard work and self-reflection through solitude took hold around 1796.[22]

Thus, the idea of the modern American prison was born (some say in Franklin's living room, though I would call that hyperbole based on other accounts[23]). What is most notable and distinct about these prisons is the shift from corporal punishment to imprisonment, which we still see today. After some iterations, prison reformers found that the "Auburn system," first implemented in a New York state prison of the same name, was the most effective solution to help reform criminals. In this system, inmates were, for the first time, housed in separate cells in order that they could reflect on their pasts, and were only brought together to do manual labor. The entire prison was also run as a silent operation, in an almost monastic sense (also an influence of the Pennsylvania Quakers).[24]

In an account from prison reformer and Auburn system champion Louis Dwight, upon his visit to the prison in 1829:

> The whole establishment, from the gate to the sewer, is a specimen of neatness. The unremitted industry, the entire subordination and subdued feeling of the convicts, has probably no parallel among an equal number of criminals. In their solitary cells they spend the night, with no other book but the Bible, and at sun-rise they proceed, in military order, under the eye of the turnkeys, in solid columns, with the lock march, to their workshops; thence, in the same order, at the hour of breakfast, to the common hall, where they partake of their wholesome and frugal meal, in silence. Not even a whisper is heard; though the silence is such, that a whisper might be heard through the whole apartment. The convicts are seated, in single file, at narrow tables, with their backs towards the center, so that there can be no interchange of signs. If one has more food than he wants, he raises his left hand; and if another has less, he raises his right hand, and the waiter changes it, When they have done eating, the ringing of a little bell, of the softest sound, they rise from the table, form the solid columns, and return, under the eye of the turnkeys, to the work-shops.[25]

## THE NINETEENTH CENTURY

> The brackish water that we drink Creeps with a loathsome slime,
> And the bitter bread they weigh in Scales
> Is full of chalk and lime, And Sleep will not lie down, but
> Walks Wild-eyed, and cries to Time
>
> —Oscar Wilde, *The Ballad of Reading Gaol*, 1898[26]

Reading this passage from Oscar Wilde, one would probably be surprised to know that during the Victorian Era, prisons in England saw marked improvement in the diet of prisoners, as well as more general prison reform. Taste, or flavor, however, really improved very little, so Wilde's text holds true to the experience, especially in its figurative undertones of depression.

"Reform in the nineteenth century was fragmented and came in waves" and was not always universal, since many prisons were still overseen individually by various townships.[27] Certainly at the early part of the Victorian narrative, food was still considered as part of punishment to inmates, but Howard's ideas seem to have resonated insofar as there was much more consistent rationing, beyond just bread and water, consisting at times of meat, potatoes, "hog gruel," and broth with vegetables.[28]

A central part of the motivation for this new regimen was, as Howard had hoped, to not let these men waste away to worthlessness in a prison complex, for if they did happen to get out, it would be much to society's advantage to have healthy citizens able to work and contribute to society. So, in a major sense, this is really the first *practice* of food being connected with a *form* of rehabilitation rather than solely with punishment. Coupled with this, we see a newfound recognition of the connection between disease, health, and food. Many of the "prison dietaries" reflected the changing scientific and, more specifically, nutritional knowledge of the day which was proliferating like crazy. Attempts to prevent scurvy, dysentery, and outbreaks of "gaol fever" all were reflected in changing prison diets of the time.

The advent of the Industrial Revolution, population changes, and overall technological and scientific advances led to many nutritional speculations and schools of thought.

> Most aspects of the social human condition were undergoing complex and often contradictory transformations, and food was no exception. Quackery and misinformation competed for authority. But by the end of the century, key contestants were traditional female herbal wisdoms of health and diet, and the developing male, scientifically-schooled and licensed, medical profession.[29]

The Victorian-era prison in England became the ultimate Petri dish or control group for a nutritional experiment. Consider it: where else did you have a group of men, at least minimally similar in physiology, with the same regimen and diet and lifestyle, in a confined setting to study and consider for lengthy periods of time? Many Victorian pioneering nutrition scientists used prisons as a means by which to study nutrition, and these studies of prison dietaries had implications for nutrition beyond the prison walls: "...the studies...not only led to improved knowledge of nutrient needs, but also to the overturning of a current basic dogma in nutritional science, and to the first estimate of the energetic efficiency of human muscles."[30]

The central tenant of the gaol diet became to create a ration-based diet based on the premise of not emaciating the prisoners, but also not offering them any extravagances. Simply put, the goal (within the gaol) was to maintain the minimum amount of nutrition to allow them to come out of prison (or even while in prison) able to work and perform hard labor, but at the same time to not offer up any luxuries.[31] Though prisoners were not treated very well on the whole and the food was really mediocre at best, we at least see some glimpse of a connection between the ideas of reforming citizens using diet in order to help them stay on the proper side of prison walls. The Victorian era saw a surge in social welfare in general and this is mirrored very clearly in prison reform.

But is this truly a show of hope for the inmates' futures and a first glimpse at an idea of rehabilitation, tied up intricately with food? There is something poignant in the Victorian struggle, especially for those interested in prison reform, because it speaks to the spirit of the age: It is precisely in this vacillation of the populace between wanting to help and wanting to punish that we see the most interesting narrative about prison food emerge. Within these struggles surrounding prison diet, the story of a society, of a culture, of a state comes through: in the age of newfound technology, the Industrial Revolution, and science, we see, as Michel Foucault seems to claim, a confusion about where to place the body and how exactly to treat it. And, with this, what goes in it.

This struggle is best illustrated in Foucault's monumental work, *Discipline and Punish: The Birth of the Prison*, in which he explicates articulately this precise struggle, eloquating this bi-focular view society had of the prisoner—on the one hand, as rejected citizen yet poor hapless soul in need of help on the other:

> Hence an ambiguity in popular attitudes: on the one hand, the criminal—especially when he happened to be a smuggler or a peasant who had fled from the exactions of a master—benefited from a spontaneous wave of sympathy: his acts of violence were seen descending directly from old struggles. On the other hand, a man who, under cover of an illegality accepted by the population, committed crimes at the expense of this population, the vagrant beggar, for example who had robbed and murdered, easily became the object of a special hate: he had redirected upon the least favoured illegality that was integral to their conditions of existence. Thus there grew up around crimes a network of glorification and blame; effective help and fear alternated with regard to this shifting population, which one knew was very near, but from which one felt that crime could emerge. Popular illegality enveloped a whole nucleus of criminality that was both its extreme form and its internal danger.[32]

Returning to nineteenth-century ideas on food and nutrition in prisons, the most common things consumed in English prisons seem to have been bread, water, various meats, broth, hot gruel, potatoes, and, more rarely, cheese, oranges, and soups; even cocoa shows up here and there.[33] Generally, prisoners were served two, but more commonly three, meals per day: breakfast, dinner, and supper. Complaints about the food in the gaols were not uncommon. As one can imagine, these were not the finest quality meats, stews, and produce. As Carpenter notes, "Some of the writings of ex-prisoners suggest that what they actually received was very different: 'On tearing the potatoes in half the interior was often found to be a mass of

A stereoscopic view card of the dining hall at the notorious Sing Sing Prison in upstate New York, in the nineteenth century. *Source*: New York Public Library.

foul, black, spongy disease' and 'I used to have to hold my nose when I tried to eat the meat.'"[34] Other accounts reflect similar displeasure at the offerings in prisons: "But of all the words which prisoners use to convey something of the quality of their bread, 'sawdust' is the most prevalent; 'the bread was quite uneatable. If it had been of sawdust flavored with road sweepings it could not have tasted worse.'"[35] There seems to be just no freshness or care for spoilage at these institutions. The descriptions become even more horrific:

> Then there was a "meat" soup. "A pint of what was called beef soup was served up to William Lovett and his fellow Chartists [presumably at Millbank Prison]. . . . They felt compelled to include it in a petition of complaint they addressed to Parliament, on the grounds that 'there was no other appearance of meat than some slimy, stringy particles, which, hanging about the wooden spoon, so offended your petitioners' stomachs that they were compelled to forgo eating it.'"[36]

American prison food in the nineteenth century is harder to find information about, but one rumor that comes up often is that on the New England shores washed so many lobster so often that prisoners in nineteenth-century Northeastern American prisons were often fed lobster day in and day out. This assertion seems valid; an entry about the history of lobster, found on History.com, says, "Dirt-cheap because they were so copious, lobsters were routinely fed to prisoners, apprentices, slaves and children during the colonial era and beyond."[37] But in a book entirely dedicated to the crustacean as a delicacy called *Lobster: A Global History*, the author quotes food historian Kathleen Curtin as saying "one of the most persistent and oft re-peated food myths . . . is about laws being enacted to protect prisoners/servants from eating lobster more than three times a week—it never happened. [There is] no shred of documentation there."[38] Other accounts of nineteenth-century American prisons paint a bleak picture, "incoming prisoners were often served bread and water until they had earned the right for such luxuries as meat and cheese."[39]

Not all food served was considered to be terrifyingly horrific, and in fact, there are accounts of prisoners sometimes calling bread "excellent" and cocoas "deli-cious," but on the whole was a general sense of tastelessness. Even descriptions of the water are at times enough to make one's stomach turn.

State Prison Greenwich Village, New York, 1801. *Source*: New York Public Library.

## RATION: THE TWENTIETH CENTURY

He suffers nothing but pain. After two hours, the felt is removed, for at that point the man has no more energy for screaming. Here at the head of the bed warm rice pudding is put in this electrically heated bowl. From this the man, if he feels like it, can help himself to what he can lap up with his tongue. No one passes up this opportunity. I don't know of a single one, and I have had a lot of experience. He first loses his pleasure in eating around the sixth hour.

—Franz Kafka, *In the Penal Colony*, 1914[40]

In 1925, an English Prison Commission outlined a major tenet for prison reform, stating, "We desire to urge, as a matter of paramount importance, that every inch of available ground should be cultivated and used for the production of vegetables . . . and of herbs for flavoring."[41] The profundity of such a statement really gave hope to an idea of mass improvement in distribution, nutrition, and quantity in prison food diets in England during the twentieth century.

Nutrition became even more important in daily life and the English government began more frequent and diligent prison visits, with commissions and recommendations cropping up here and there to improve the life of the prisoner, especially with regard to diet. In this period, we see the introduction of fresh vegetables and beans to the prison diet and the "ration scale" (a means for providing equal distribution among prisoners) was utilized almost universally.[42] "Men in convict prisons were provided with, on average, 3,633 calories a day. Their diet was more varied, containing pork soup and beef once a week. Women in local prisons were provided with food containing on average 2,456 calories a day. As the reader can most likely deduce from today's calorie recommendations (average 2,000 per day), this was ample energy intake per prisoner, and it was found that most prisoners did gain weight while incarcerated.[43] Despite being (maybe overly) ample in energy, the quality of the food still left something to be desired.

There was still evidence of "punishment diets" for the grosser offenders, of which there were two different varieties: "One which lasted three days or less and consisted of bread and water and the other which lasted for twenty-one days or less and consisted of bread, water, potatoes and porridge (Prison Commission, 1925)"[44] indicating that there was still little hope for using diet as a means to true rehabilitation.

The implementation of prison gardens for food cultivation during the early and mid-twentieth century was more interesting. "In-house agriculture was seen as a way of significantly increasing the amount of fresh produce in the diet at little cost. Any surplus could be passed on to other prisons. Suggested vegetables for cultivation included potatoes, spinach, kale, cabbage, watercress, carrots, onions, parsnips and swedes."[45] Cultivation was used as a means for cheaply producing more food commodities but no indication is given that inmates participated in or benefited from gardening themselves.

What this seems to purport is a direction toward a consideration of diet and rehabilitation as not incongruous. Many prisoners were considered even healthier, due to their increase in weight and therefore "strength" when they came out of prison than when they went in. On the whole, the inclination of the governmental implementation of prison diet reform seems to be more capitalistic than a wholehearted idea of rehabilitation, insofar as they still wanted the former inmates to come out as stand-up citizens able for *work*. Little or no consideration is given to any degree of mental reform where diet is concerned. As was the fashion of the day, food was used as medicine for bodily ailments but a healthy diet does not seem to generally appear in a discussion of mental rehabilitation. Prisoners, and reform, are seen more for their use-value or utility than any sentient being with a sense of purpose beyond work—to even consider that to be healthy in body is central to being healthy in mind seems a stretch for even the most astute prison reformers, who for so many years saw prisoners more as workhorses than human beings capable of reform.

Further, the ration system itself can be considered from two sides: it created an egalitarian system of food distribution, but at the same time discounted any individuality. When you discount even basic physiological variables, you run the risk of malnutrition, plain and simple. It seems the introduction of fresh fruits and vegetables, a tasty and improved diet, was relatively short-lived in English prisons, with the 1960s and 1970s being probably the closest to "good" that prison diets got: "By 1973, it was reported that there was greater variety of food with more fresh fruit and vegetables, and poultry was on the menu for the first time (Home Office, 1974). By 1974, a vegetarian diet had been introduced."[46] That is not to say that if you were going to be a prisoner, the 1970s would have been the ideal time to be one—the food was often called "bland," was cooked far ahead of eating, and the ration scale was still in place (through the 1990s), but there was a short-lived time of marked improvement in prison diets.

In America, twentieth-century prison food seemed to take an upswing in parallel with its English counterparts, with reports of the food at the famous prison of Alcatraz being relatively good. A menu from 1946 has potato chowder, bacon jambalaya, and beef pot pie on it to name a few things. When I visited the island, the chow hall seemed airy, spacious, and I could imagine it being a bustling, lively place at one time. However, other accounts of Alcatraz say that they deliberately fed their prisoners upward of 5,000 calories a day and gave them little exercise time to make them lethargic and complacent.[47]

# 3

# The Business of Prison Food

The cost to produce a school meal, according to the School Nutrition Association, is around $2.30 for the average lunch.[1] Our American prison system feeds almost 2 million inmates a full three meals per day on around two to four dollars. Without delving into the crazy parallels between school meals and prison food, this statistic indicates how cheaply prison meals are made. If we as a nation have been appalled of late at the nutritionally inadequate and paltry meals we provide schoolchildren, what does it say that we feed prisoners (mostly grown men) three meals per day for the same amount as one school lunch? The fact is that $2.30 is pretty much average, but as this chapter will discuss, that number can dip below $1.75 in some cases. Fascinatingly, prisons are an industry that remains untouched by national economic stability. In 2009 alone, when most industries were in a slump, the prison industry brought in $34.4 billion in revenues.[2]

Running a prison requires a stunning amount of organization and budgeting, given the sheer number of people and services being administered. Correctional facilities are, at the end of the day, businesses with budgets, and foodservice is one large component of them. Prisons and jails are run by local, state, or federal governments, and occasionally by private owners. In all of these cases, the aim is, as with all businesses or governmental organizations, to keep costs low while meeting necessary requirements. Of course, a key difference between a typical business that provides food and a prison or jail is that the aim is not maximum satisfaction and return customers. The aim is to meet the nutritional requirements put forth by the state and create safely prepared meals that satiate prisoners without too many frills or disruptions.

This chapter outlines the ways in which prison food is administered, by whom, and at what cost, as well as the corruption that surrounds keeping correctional facility costs at an absolute minimum. A final component addressed is the creation, within correctional facilities, of a micro-economy based partially on food. Part of the life of any prisoner is procuring tender, often in the form of food or goods, to be traded or sold on the black market. This business is thriving, serious, and revolves enormously around food.

## CORRECTIONAL FOOD BUDGETS

American prisons are often associated with shocking statistics about the price per prisoner they pay to host our nation's incarcerated population, with some prisons and jails, such as New York City, paying up to $168,000 per year per prisoner.[3] These incredible amounts have even sparked some to write about the notion of a "million dollar block": a place in an inner-city in which people from that block bounce in and out of prison so much that the block can cost the city and state up to $1 million a year.[4] The Vera Institute for Justice states in its report, "The Price of Prisons," that the total per-inmate cost averages $31,286 nationwide and ranged from $14,603 in Kentucky to $60,076 in New York with the average price per inmate being generally lower in states with more crowded prisons.[5] It is very common to hear about what such an enormous incarcerated population costs taxpayers, particularly in an election year and with a number of people trying to shock the population into understanding how massive our incarceration problem is, but what is less common is to dig into what those numbers mean. Ta-Nehisi Coates recently summed up the role of correctional facilities in an incredible article on race and incarceration for the *Atlantic*, saying, "At a cost of $80 billion a year, American correctional facilities are a social-service program—providing health care, meals, and shelter for a whole class of people."[6] Given the amount of services and the number of people serviced, is it surprising that these numbers are so staggering? With the corrections population topping that of the population of America's fourth-largest city, it is no wonder that a huge budget is required to run these facilities.

While the cost of prison to our country each year remains shockingly high, the cost per meal per prisoner remains incredibly low, despite large increases in the cost of food. Though the price of fresh fruits and vegetables, and nourishing items such as milk has skyrocketed over the last decade, the price per meal paid per prisoner at correctional facilities has, on the whole, not risen with the times. In fact, the

*LA Times* published an article in 2002 explaining that the price paid per prisoner per meal had not increased in fourteen years.[7] Food budgets for correctional facilities are part of larger budgeting systems, and foodservice providers at correctional facilities are expected to meet a per person per day cost for food. This cost varies from facility to facility, but generally hovers between $1.85 and more than three times that much (if a special dietary restriction is involved).[8]

Food in prison is often run by the facility itself and not outsourced, as may be the common conception. While contracted foodservice providers do service many facilities nationwide, many prison kitchens are run in-house under the leadership of a foodservice administrator or director, who typically manages all of the procedures of the kitchen facility at a correctional institution. This person, along with a couple of managers, is responsible for ordering, receiving, storing, preparing, and serving the food along with maintaining an efficient budget, cost tracking, and managing a kitchen staff. In addition to running the business side of managing a kitchen, the foodservice administrator must grapple with upholding food safety standards and ensuring that nutritional guidelines are met. It is a high-stress, high-pressure job.

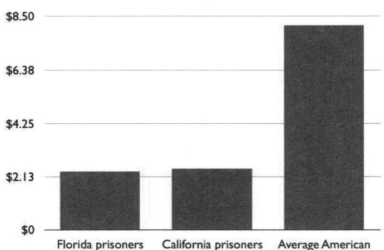

St. Petersburg Times, June 17, 2002; Los Angeles Times, June 17, 2002; Calculation: USDA Per Capita Food Expenditures, Table 15

The Prison Index

*Source*: "Daily Cost to Feed Prisoners and the Average American." Prison Policy Initiative. Accessed May 24, 2015. www.prisonpolicy.org/graphs/foodcosts.html.

Prison food is based on the "flash-frozen" or "blast chill" method, meaning essentially that the food is mostly prepared at an off-site facility, shipped frozen to the prisons or jails, and simply reheated. According to the *New York Times*, this method was invented in Trenton, New Jersey, in the 1980s to decrease cost and increase efficiency: "Under that system, food for a seven-day week is cooked within a 40-hour, five-day week. What is not used immediately is blast-chilled to approximately 45 degrees in an insulated 250-cubic-foot steel cabinet."[9] This method has largely continued to the present day due to its ease in budgeting and preparation.

It was interesting to hear about the precision with which food must be served in order to prevent any sort of inmate discord or frustration. Inmates are well aware of what the menu says regarding how much they will be served and what that amount looks like. Former Arizona State Prison System foodservice supervisor Jennifer Waite spoke of the rigidity necessary surrounding portioning and service: "inmates know the correct serving size for each item. Inconsistent portion sizes can lead to brawls in the chow hall if an inmate looks over to find a double-helping on another guy's tray, especially if the inmates in question are of two different races."[10] Another practice intended to cut costs and maximize use of food purchased is the "re-rack" system. "Under the re-rack system, 95 percent of uneaten food is not thrown out, but rather frozen and re-served up to seven days after it was first distributed to the inmates."[11] Inmates, not surprisingly, catch on very quickly to the fact that they are being served repurposed fare, and it does not sit or settle well with them.

## PRISON PRIVATIZATION

Prison privatization refers to correctional facilities that are not run by the federal, state, or local government, but are in fact outsourced as a contract to a corporation and run by that corporation. In the United States, there are public and privately run prisons on both the state and federal level. "On average, state prisons run at 110 percent capacity, and federal prisons at 137 percent. It is much cheaper for states to contract with a private prison rather than build a new one."[12] The government enters into a contractual agreement with them and pays the corporation a certain amount of money each year (generally a price per prisoner) to administer corrections for these inmates. That being said, that is only one facet of understanding how prisons have "become privatized" over the last forty years. In addition to entire correctional facilities being run by corporations, there are a number of other services that have been outsourced to private companies who contract and work within publicly run facilities. Tracy F. H. Chang and Douglas E. Thompkins explain:

The idea and practice of "privatization," delegating public duties to private organizations, gained popularity when [President Ronald] Reagan gained electoral support by advocating the idea of small government and free market economy. Concurrently, the rising prison population was overcrowding correctional facilities and consuming government budgets nationwide.[13]

In the *Atlantic*, Eric Schlosser coined the term "prison-industrial complex" to describe the upsurge in interest the private sector has had in the business of corrections. He says, "The rationale for private prisons is that government monopolies such as old-fashioned departments of corrections are inherently wasteful and inefficient, and the private sector, through competition for contracts, can provide much better service at a much lower cost."[14] This combination has made many Americans very wealthy through the construction of prison facilities, vending, surveillance, technology, prison food, medical services, and such things as phone service. Unfortunately, as Schlosser also points out, this has led to corporations being in bed with the government, and job performance is often poor, particularly when it comes to food. Chang and Thompkins point out:

The soaring prison population inspired entrepreneurs seeking business opportunities. Corporations began to seek multi-million dollar contracts with state governments in constructing, managing, and operating prisons. Federal and state governments, and private sectors began to expand the employment of inmates for profitable production and services.[15]

Furthermore, "The industry's giants—Corrections Corporation of America, The GEO Group, and Management and Training Corp.—have spent at least $45 million combined on campaign donations and lobbyists at the state and federal level in the last decade,"[16] according to the Associated Press.

## CONTRACTED FOODSERVICE PROVIDERS

Contracted foodservice providers are utilized by both publicly run and privatized prisons, depending on the facility. Contractors often secure gigs when they come in offering to slash budgetary costs and provide meals at the lowest possible price, taking the burden from top management. Their contracts are generally lengthy, at minimum around three years. Contracts are often statewide, servicing all the facilities of that given state, with the governor of an individual state being the decider on whom the contract will go to and at what price.[17] The additional advantage of working with a contracted service provider for meals and commissary is their purchasing power: These are generally corporations buying en masse, leveraging deals with food distributors to get the maximum deal possible on food goods. It is the simple principle of economies-of-scale: A single facility, or even a few, would not have this leveraging power on their own.

Former Arizona State Prison System foodservice supervisor Jennifer Waite said that contractors are often responsible for shouldering all facets of food provided in correctional facilities:

> Though the inmates do most of the work, and the correctional officers are there to maintain order, it is civilian contractors who are often responsible for every aspect of the meal preparation: inmate training, adherence to recipes, ensuring food safety standards are met, theft prevention, portion control and general quality of service. Portion control is of utmost importance when preparing food for 800 inmates, as whatever is in the freezer is likely all there is.[18]

A few contracted food providers reign in the corrections industry, including Aramark, A'Viands Food and Service Management, ABL Management, Canteen Correctional Services, and Trinity Services Group.[19] Often, these providers will take care of managing the chow hall meals of breakfast, lunch, and dinner, but will also be in charge of stocking and vending the commissary with food and items. According to their Web site, Trinity Services Group has contracts with more than four hundred jails and prisons in forty-five states, Puerto Rico, and the US Virgin Islands.[20] Aramark, a well-known provider of institutional food across correctional facilities, universities, workplaces, convention centers, sports arenas, and hospitals, does not state the number of contracts they have in corrections facilities on their Web site, but instead says they provide over 380 million meals to correctional facilities each year.[21] Both contractors' Web sites purport to understand the way in which food contributes to a safe facility environment with regard to corrections. Aramark's tagline is "Serving Up the Right Meals for a Safer Environment," while Trinity claims to understand that mealtime "plays a critical role in the overall stability of a secure facility."[22] But when it comes down to it, nothing about the food they provide seems to reinforce this in particular, given the endless string of complaints provided by inmates as well as the often-cited issues of failing to provide healthy, safe food (more on this in a bit). As with many corporations, these companies seem to be getting away with what they can and providing the absolute base amount of nutrition and calories to get by. They increase their bottom line and generally go unchallenged in this space, because prisoners and their grievances are so easily overlooked.

Foodservice in prisons is highly unregulated, to put it simply. Nutritional standards (discussed in the next chapter) and food safety are regulated only by the facilities themselves, save for when an inmate is actually able to get to the point of filing a lawsuit that then is followed through and investigated. Generally speaking, correctional facilities follow the food safety regulations of their jurisdiction, but on the whole no particular designated governmental agency is sent to inspect or regulate them. Unlike the places where you dine in your city or town, correctional facilities almost always fall out of the jurisdiction of health inspection by the city or state government because they are not "food establishments."[23]

Vendors' links to universities and other facilities frequented by the public is also to the public's interest. The providers of prison food are often the very corporations that are servicing the food programs at many educational institutions, sports arenas, government buildings, and hospitals across the country. Aramark alone services thousands of universities, including the one I attended. It does not take a lot of imagination to conjure that the distinction between the food sourced and provided for correctional facilities by a corporation such as Aramark would not differ that greatly from that which gets sent to the schools.

Who is pocketing the money from running correctional facilities and how are they doing it? Food is certainly one way.

## CORRUPTION

Prisons are paid for mostly by state and federal taxes, and therefore the incentive to cut costs and skim extra revenue off the top is huge for prison administrators. Often, a warden's salary is directly correlated to how much penny pinching he or she can do to keep overhead low, and food is a massive space to cut cost. The privatization of prison and jail foodservices is said to have begun in Alabama. According to David Reutter:

> Over 70 years ago, Alabama passed a law that provided county sheriffs with $1.75 a day per jail prisoner to cover the cost of their meals. While the law went into effect in 1939, it is still in use today. Under that system, Alabama sheriffs are personally responsible for paying for prisoners' food, but are allowed to keep any excess funds if they can feed prisoners for less than the payments they receive from the state.[24]

That means, so confusingly, that a sheriff is given the entire foodservice budget in a given year and is asked to purchase the food for the facility himself. Ostensibly, this was an incentive for sheriffs and wardens to cut costs, but why? And at what true price? Naturally, complications have arisen with stories of absolutely corrupt wardens and sheriffs pocketing money at the expense of prisoner health and well-being.

In one of the most egregious examples in recent history, an Alabama Sheriff named Greg Bartlett began feeding prisoners such insanely cheap meals that he was able to skim over $200,000 in money allocated toward food, until a federal lawsuit, filed by prisoners Johnny Maynor and Anthony Murphree, uncovered the truth about how Bartlett was saving so much. *Prison Legal News* online, discusses the case:

> What the district court found was deplorable. For breakfast, prisoners received a serving of unsweetened grits or oatmeal, a slice of bread and half an egg or less. Lunch consisted of either two baloney sandwiches or two sandwiches with a dab of peanut butter, plus a small bag of corn chips. For dinner prisoners were served either chicken livers, meat patties or two hot dogs, either slaw or onions, beans or mixed vegetables, and a slice of bread.[25]

Bartlett, who had been previously ordered via a Consent Decree in 2001 to begin serving "nutritionally adequate" meals, was found to have failed to do so, and therefore jailed for his violations. Perhaps what is most fascinating about the Bartlett case is that by taking $200,000 in funds for himself he was not violating any regulations—it was that he was not providing nutritionally adequate meals. I wonder what he was given to eat during his jail time!

Further corruption is often seen when foodservice workers come into facilities as contracted, part-timers making very little money at a pretty thankless job. Accounts of workers smuggling food and drugs to inmates, giving them cell phones, or engaging in illicit behavior, and even having sexual relationships or committing murder have surfaced. The *Detroit Free Press* published a 2014 account of an Aramark foodservice worker at Kinross Correctional Facility "approaching an inmate there about arranging to have another inmate killed."[26]

## CUTTING CORNERS

Cutbacks, cutbacks, cutbacks. One of the most frequently used words that I read while researching the topic of prison food was cutbacks. Correctional institutions are constantly coming up with new ways to save pennies—"taxpayer dollars"— and food is an easy target in the budget. In recent headlines, claims that "Obama pulled pork" off the menu of federal correctional facilities were true, for about a week. In October of 2015, the president's administration, in conjunction with the Federal Bureau of Prisons, removed pork from all federal penitentiaries, saying that pork was undesired by inmates who sought healthier lifestyles.[27] It also helped streamline the issue with kosher and nonkosher meals by being able to serve everyone the same thing more frequently. After a firestorm erupted and the National Pork Producers Council said the claims that prisoners did not want bacon were unfounded, the government put it back on the menu.[28] According to the *Washington Post* article on its reinstatement, the national menu had already eliminated sausages, bacon, and pork chops with the only pork-centric dish remaining on the menu being pork roast.

Despite the booming nature of the prison industry in general, corporations that run the prisons (as well as the state and federal institutions that run them) are always trying to save costs, and often this means cutting corners and causing inmate unrest. The transition from publicly run facilities to private ones often does not come without complaints and frustrations due to the way Aramark and other contracted foodservice companies cut corners. My Google alert for "prison food" comes through almost every single day with a new issue, story, or lawsuit about a company not living up to adequate standards. *Prison Legal News* online compiled a number of grievances raised about Aramark:

- Foodservices at both prisons were provided by Aramark, which believes its meals are the best thing since sliced bread. "It's a tremendous piece of inmate happiness," said Laurie Stolen, the inmate services director for Larimer County, who didn't indicate whether she ate the food prepared at the facility.
- Many prisoners who partake of Aramark meals, however, are not happy. "We used to get two slices of bread, then we got one. We only got half a scoop of vegetables instead of a full scoop," said Angela Sewel, incarcerated at Wisconsin's Taycheedah Correctional Institution, which contracts with Aramark. "They ran out of milk . . . the soda was being watered down. They really cut back."
- Pennsylvania's Allegheny County Jail contracted with Aramark until August 2007. When interviewed by a news reporter, one prisoner held up an orange slice of cheese and remarked, "I don't think you could melt this with a blast furnace." Other prisoners said things improved after a new contractor, Canteen, took over. "You can melt this cheese," a prisoner said about Canteen's fare.
- In Clayton County, Georgia, prisoners went three months without hot food—from October 2009 to January 22, 2010—after the pressure cookers in the jail's kitchen went out. Most of the ovens and skillets were inoperable, too. Prisoners received cold pasta, bologna, cereal, sandwiches, fruit, and hard-boiled eggs. "This is the fourth day I've had cold noodles," said Clayton County jail prisoner Joquayla Perry, who was five weeks pregnant. "This is what we eat every day, and it's nasty."[29]

In recent years, some wardens of jails, prisons, and other correctional facilities across the country have made the bold move of reducing the number of meals served per day from three to just two. And the change has not gone unnoticed. In Georgia, when the Gordon County Jail in Calhoun switched to this practice, inmates were not just upset—they were hungry: "One prisoner said he eased hunger pangs by eating toothpaste. One complained he got so little food that he trembled at night in his cell. Another filed grievance after grievance, each consisting of a single word: 'Hungry.'"[30]

Cutbacks are not just in quantity of meals, but also in quality or type of meals and ingredients. Accounts of reduction in milk, fresh fruit, and meat abound.[31] In Arizona in 2013, a notoriously hard sheriff named Joe Arpaio who runs the Maricopa County jail system took the year to phase out meat and save approximately $100,000 a year.[32] He replaced the meat with soy-laden products in order to meet protein requirements. But at what other cost? Inmate unrest, as discussed, is directly tied to changes in routine. It seems worth mentioning that this same sheriff also makes all inmates wear pink underwear, pay for their own meals, and many are forced to sleep in tents out in the Arizona heat, prompting the *New York Times* to deem him "America's Worst Sheriff."[33] And because these things get muddled in terminology, I will gently remind readers that jails are merely stopgaps for those accused of crimes, innocent until proven guilty, under our Constitution. So, one wonders why the incredibly harsh conditions for *potential* criminals? While the courts have not ignored Sheriff Arpaio, and he has been the subject of many investigations surrounding the way he runs his jail system, he is (at time of writing) still sheriff and running for another election to the position, at age eighty-three. Similar attempts to take meat off the menu have resulted in lawsuits and frustration among inmates, using the Eighth Amendment argument, saying the soy was dangerous to their health.[34] These seem to have been widely dismissed and soy is often cited on menus, as it makes accommodating special diets easier by simply feeding everyone the same thing (meatless, dairyless, etc.).

In 2008 in Florida, where the company is headquartered, Aramark was running all of the correctional foodservice programs when it came under investigation for allegations that it was pocketing millions of dollars by charging for meals that it never served. Additionally, the company had served a chili meal in April of that year which made 277 inmates ill, obviously raising questions about the health and safety measures taken by the company.[35] The contract between the state of Florida was signed under the governorship of Governor Jeb Bush, a staunch Republican. Investigations into the company and its services in Florida Corrections did not come into question until Bush left office and was replaced by Democratic Governor Charlie Crist, making many people question why Bush gave Aramark the contract in the first place and allowed the company to continue pocketing funds and taking shortcuts at the expense of taxpayers and the safety of inmates and correctional officers.[36]

In Michigan, a huge amount of news has erupted over Aramark's handling of foodservices at correctional facilities, which the company took over in early 2015 as part of a three-year contract and one that is supposed to save the state $16 million a year. Multiple accounts of maggots being found in the food, rodent-nibbled cake, serving food that had previously been thrown in the trash or spoiled food, and workers having sex with inmates and conspiring in a murder-for-hire plot surfaced and were beginning to be investigated.[37] When Aramark came under such intense fire, Michigan Governor Rick Snyder, under pressure from his constituency, decided to end the contract the state had with the foodservice provider, though reports say it was a "mutual agreement" with Aramark claiming that the political climate was too highly charged to refute "repeated false claims."[38] Snyder handed the new $158 million contract (for three years) over to Trinity Services Group. At time of writing, the saga surrounding abysmal prison food in Michigan continues as advocates for ethical treatment of prisoners along with two state legislators have introduced legislation to require inspection of institutions' kitchens by the local county health department, similar to what is done for restaurants.[39] When *Vice* had someone within a Michigan prison write about what they had been eating under the Aramark contract, they described the food by saying:

> there's no imagining the cartoonish dishes that landed in front of us, like bologna soup. I couldn't have known beforehand that "meatballs" in fluorescent gray sauce would be cause for excitement because they were the best thing rolling out of the kitchen . . . the dinner line ran at 3:30 PM, at which time we received four slices of damp, white bread packed with a piece of sweaty bologna and a couple cookies. A small snack is the only thing one eats between the 10:30 AM lunch and 4:30 AM breakfast.[40]

## THE OTHER BUSINESS OF PRISON FOOD

As *Business Insider* put it, a thriving economy exists within prisons due to "The isolated consumer base, the high demand for goods, [and] the excruciatingly limited supply—it's a hothouse of entrepreneurial finesse, extreme risk—and obscene returns."[41] Prisoners use their correctional officers as mules for contraband, sizing up each officer, getting friendly with them, and bribing the corrupt ones to bring them high-value items such as drugs and cell phones (probably the two most coveted items). Generally, prisoners do not have cash sent to them, save when they need to pay off an officer, but they use a credit card that is prepaid (commonly a Green Dot Reloadable card) in order to pay each other.[42] "In order to conduct business with one another, the prisoners have credit cards—most of them use Green Dot Reloadable prepaid cards, which their loved ones can purchase at drugstores."[43] But at the same time as these items come in through purchase with money, they immediately acquire their own "prison value" in a micro-economy based solely, as stated before, on limited supply.

There are rules against trading of any kind within these walls, of course. But rules in prison are meant to be ignored, even by most guards. It's hard to imagine that there's a jail anywhere without some system of trade. Not even a society of disposable humans can shun an economy.

This past week I bought a set of bed sheets, some tape to fix my headphones, and some contraband vegetables. Altogether I owe about twelve dollars out and, generally speaking, convict bill collectors aren't very civil. Even if I was willing to tough it without commissary for myself, debts must be paid because I simply love keeping my blood in the convenient container it comes in, so I stay diligent about paying my arrears.[44]

Food takes on incredible value in prison by turning into a tradeable and sellable commodity. My friend wrote to me about one of the most astounding examples of this he had witnessed: "I once saw a guy pay 4 books of stamps ($25) for a small pouch of shrimp that certainly was not worth $3."[45] In one account of "getting a hustle" published on *The Marshall Project*, inmate Patrick Larmour describes all sorts of lengths and means by which he and fellow inmates make a buck or get the stuff they really want, including cell phones, cigarettes, drugs, and food. Inmates called "Vultures" scoop up the tobacco spit out onto the ground from correctional officers, dry it out to roll into a cigarette, and sell them for about $10 a pop.[46] Curiously, Larmour was most impressed with the creativity that comes with "the hustle." As he describes it, "The surprising thing is, the majority of hustles in prison are positive. I've seen my fellow inmates carve bars of soap into beautiful sculptures or draw portraits and then sell them to their neighbors. Others wash and iron clothes, sew, repair electronics, mend damaged shoes, run sports pools, do legal work, operate stores, and even fashion TV antennas from paper clips. Some polish stones they find on the yard and make them into necklaces or furniture; some draw birthday cards; and some sell homemade burritos and candy."[47]

Everything in prison has its prison price, based on the micro-economy of that institution, as established over years and years of inmates developing it. At Rikers Island in New York, a particularly notorious jail (where those accused of crimes can end up staying for up to a year awaiting trial), this micro-economy is in full effect. As one inmate describes to *The Marshall Project*:

> I gave a bag of mayonnaise for a week of phone calls. It was like ten phone calls or something like that. There are things in commissary that are hard to find. So when they have mayonnaise, you try to stock up on it. BBQ chips are more popular than the other chips, they run out really quick, so you can trade those for phone calls. Everyone does very exact calculations. Like a pack of mayo costs ten cents and a phone call costs $1.50 for a short phone call. And usually the deals are as close to one-to-one as is possible. A lot of people give away phone calls because they don't have anyone to call. The phones are probably the biggest source of drama.[48]

Former foodservice supervisor Waite spoke of prisoners wanting to get their hands on some "luxury items" or less accessible foods, and one way was to work in the prison kitchen:

> A "resource" is a common name for the instant-breakfast packets that are doled out to a few inmates who may need a boost in calories, or who cannot ingest solid food. These packets are given with milk to those determined by medical to need them. Resources and milk are very hot commodities, as both pack a protein boost difficult to attain through other prison foods. Those who work out a lot, and who strive to get bigger while incarcerated, will pay several dollars a pop to get their hands on these items, and those getting them for their medical diets will often go without and stockpile them, selling them later at pure profit.[49]

## CONCLUSION

Perhaps it is not surprising that the more general food movement does not actively seek to help correct the quality and condition of prison food, but failing to recognize its continued and vast contribution to the larger food system, based just on sheer volume alone, is an oversight. Prison food and its sources, as well as the often corrupt providers that hold a monopoly on contracts, purchase, prepare, and distribute enough food to correctional facilities each year to move the food system needle. Prisons and jails combined serve an estimated 6.6 million meals every day to the over 2.2 million incarcerated.

# 4

# Sample Menus, Nutritional Standards, and Special Diets

In the United States, "Corrections" for criminals runs along a continuum from punishment to sustenance to rehabilitation. Food is no exception. This chapter explores the dietary and sanitary guidelines placed on prison food, and how they are met. A look at sample menus in congruence with nutritional standards will be shown. Worth noting is how fluidly interpreted these menu items are. Additionally, we will explore what it means to have a religious or other dietary restriction behind bars, how this is accommodated, and how food is again simultaneously a convener and separator.

## CALORIES AND NUTRITIONAL REQUIREMENTS

Everything about prison and jail food is fixed: Prisoners eat a fixed menu on a fixed schedule sitting in a seat that is fixed to the ground, likely sitting next to the same fixed group of people every single day. It is not easy for an inmate to deviate from the set meal save for spending a lot of money at the commissary.

For inmates in federal correctional institutions, nutritional standards are created by the Bureau of Prisons, which bases its guidelines on Dietary Reference Intakes for different population groups published by the Food and Nutrition Board of the National Academy of Sciences. These guidelines stipulate that inmates be given between 3.9 and 6.31 pounds of food per day (pre-preparation weight). As a *Slate* article on prison food clarified, "Supervised inmates typically prepare the food, so some ingredients call for heightened security. Alcohol-based flavorings, for example, must be stored in a locked cabinet, along with other 'hot items' like cloves, nutmeg, and mace (the latter two come from a plant that contains the narcotic myristicin)."[1]

Nutritional guidelines and caloric standards are typically based on the Dietary Guidelines for Americans, which are reexamined every five years and published on health.gov. That being said, there is no one set of nutritional and caloric guidelines for all correctional facilities in the United States. The Bureau of Prisons has a manual iterating certain requirements for each facility to meet for federal facilities, but they are loose and up for interpretation by each facility. The Department of Justice Food Service Manual (the most recent version found is from 2011), states that each inmate shall be "provided with nutritionally adequate meals, prepared and served in a manner that meets established Government health and safety codes."[2] Beyond this, correctional facilities are essentially required to avoid violating the Eighth Amendment, in which an inmate could incite cruel and unusual punishment. Each state, county, and even facility has its own interpretation of these guidelines, with further requirements imposed by independent certifying agencies.

Registered dietitian Barbara Wakeen has consulted on foodservice for many correctional facilities. In a June 2016 article in *Today's Dietitian* she explained that assisting facilities in their foodservice can be challenging due to lack of universal rules:

> Every facility is different when it comes to their foodservice programs. . . . What you need to do depends on the governing agency (county, state, or federal) and accreditations (American Correctional Association [ACA] and National Commission on Correctional Health Care [NCCHC]) for the facility, as well as the type of facility for which you're working. If a facility is participating in the child nutrition program, these regulations must be incorporated as well. You modify the foodservice plan depending on what the client wants and on the criteria, standards, and accreditation for each type of facility.[3]

Notice that her synopsis does not say "every state" or "every county" is different, but rather *every facility* has different guidelines. The article goes on to say that nutrient and calorie requirements are so varied that dietitian consultants do their best to help create menus that meet the needs of the tens of thousands of inmates in the system, but it is an incredible challenge to produce nutritional and calorically adequate meals that meet regional tastes and fit in budget. "As an example of how requirements can vary, California jails that fall under the Title 15 Code of Regulations have a detailed meal pattern, and macronutrient requirements and limitations; Minnesota jails have meal pattern requirements; and Ohio jails require nutritionally adequate menus," Wakeen says. "As a consultant, you work with your prison's requirements."

Generally, one salt and one pepper packet are provided, but sometimes more or less is given. Food is notoriously "bland." This is to avoid issues with inmates that suffer from hypertension (high blood pressure) or high cholesterol: If all the food is made really low in sodium, inmates with health issues will not have a problem. The other way to flavor food in the chow hall is with hot sauce, which is hugely popular if the facility allows it. Inmates will often tote bottles of hot sauce with them to and from the chow hall to spice up or cover up otherwise completely flavorless fare.

## SAMPLE MENUS

What's in a name? Well, not much when you look at correctional facility menus. On the surface, the dishes that are supposedly going to be prepared sound decent, good, even appetizing in some instances, but the way in which they are "interpreted" leaves much to be desired. As one prisoner put it when he arrived to prison, "Monday night dinner—Chicken Fried Steak. Tuesday night—Chicken Alfredo. Wednesday night—Chicken Quarters. When the guard announced over the loudspeaker, 'Gentlemen, it's CHOW TIME!' I found myself salivating over the prospect of a tasty meal, but boy, was I in for a surprise." The menu set forth and even the recipes that go with it are not what make or break correctional food to be good or bad. It truly varies from facility to facility on a number of factors, including whether or not the inmates themselves are making it, if it is contracted, and who's in charge. A former foodservice supervisor in the Arizona correctional system summed it up best when she wrote, "The quality of the prison food will always vary, based on the quality of the ingredients and the skill level of the inmates preparing the food."[4] Another typical complaint is that what is served simply disregards what is written on the menu completely. One prisoner, in a blog about Pelican Bay State Prison in California, said, "I laugh every time I see a menu, because it looks good on paper, but I know we won't see most of it. Hell, they been giving us crackers for dessert almost every night. Those are lunch crackers."[5]

Menus for federal prisons (the population of which constitutes only a tenth of the total inmate population in the United States) are produced yearly by the Bureau of Prisons (BOP), called the Certified Food Menu, and are based on a set of certified foods that can be found on an internally accessed database. The manual for foodservice, the most recent of which is a 2011 version, is posted on the BOP Web site and states that these menus will be reviewed yearly and changed based on surveys of inmates and foodservice workers.[6] According to the BOP manual, the purpose of this survey is to "assess responsiveness to inmate eating preferences, operational impact, product pricing, and nutritional content."[7] Generally, prison menus rotate on a six-week basis, though sometimes with more frequency depending on the institution. Menus must always include a flesh-free option and be able to accommodate religious restrictions.

Week 1

## Lunch & Dinner

| Sunday Lunch | Monday Lunch | Tuesday Lunch | Wednesday Lunch | Thursday Lunch | Friday Lunch | Saturday Lunch |
|---|---|---|---|---|---|---|
| ♥Scrambled Eggs | ♥Fish Tacos | Chicken Patty Sandwich | ♥Hamburger | ♥Baked Chicken | Breaded Fish Sand or | Hot Dogs (2) |
| ♥Oven Brown Potatoes | #or Soy Soft Tacos | ♥or Soy Chicken Patty | #or Soy Burger | ♥or PB & Jelly Sand (2) | ♥Baked Fish | ♥for Soy Burger w/ |
| Cream Gravy | ♥Black Beans | ♥Potato Salad | French Fries or | ♥Baked Sweet Potato | #or Soy Burger w/ | ♥WW Hamburger Bun |
| Biscuits (2) or | ♥WK Corn | ♥Pinto Beans | ♥Baked Potato | ♥Pinto Beans | Salad Dressing | Tater Tots or |
| ♥Whole Wheat Bread | ♥Flour Tortilla (2) | ♥Lettuce/Tomato/Onion | ♥Shredded Lettuce | ♥Green Beans | ♥Macaroni Salad | ♥Baked Potato |
| and Jelly (2) | ♥Shredded Lettuce | Salad Dressing | ♥Catsup & Mustard | ♥Whole Wheat Bread | ♥Green Peas | ♥Coleslaw |
| ♥Margarine Pat | Salsa | ♥WW Hamburger Bun | Pickles | ♥Margarine Pat | ♥WW Hamburger Bun | ♥Catsup & Mustard |
| ♥Fruit | ♥Margarine Pat | ♥Margarine Pat | Salad Dressing | Dessert or | ♥Margarine Pat | ♥WW Hot Dog Buns (2) |
| ♥Beverage | ♥Fruit | Dessert or | ♥WW Hamburger Bun | ♥Fruit | Tartar Sauce | ♥Margarine Pat |
|  | ♥Beverage | ♥Fruit | ♥Margarine Pat | ♥Beverage | ♥Fruit | Dessert or |
|  |  | ♥Beverage | ♥Fruit |  | ♥Beverage | ♥Fruit |
|  |  |  | ♥Beverage |  |  | ♥Beverage |

| Sunday Dinner | Monday Dinner | Tuesday Dinner | Wednesday Dinner | Thursday Dinner | Friday Dinner | Saturday Dinner |
|---|---|---|---|---|---|---|
| ♥Roast Beef | ♥Vegetable Soup | ♥Meatloaf | ♥Black Bean Soup | ♥Vegetable Soup | ♥Chicken Fried Rice | ♥Spaghetti |
| #or Cottage Cheese | ♥Chicken Salad | #or Soy Burger w/ | ♥Beef Taco Salad or | ♥Tuna Salad | # or Tofu Fried Rice | ♥w/Meat Sauce |
| ♥Baked Potato | #or Hummus | Salad Dressing | #Soy Taco Salad | #or Cheese Sand w/ | ♥Steamed Broccoli | #or Soy Spag Sauce |
| ♥Green Beans | ♥Green Peas | ♥Mashed Potatoes | Salsa | Salad Dressing | ♥Whole Wheat Bread | ♥Spinach |
| ♥Black Eyed Peas | ♥Italian Pasta Salad | Tomato Gravy | ♥Whole Wheat Bread | ♥Lettuce Leaf | ♥Margarine Pat | Garlic Bread or |
| Brown Gravy | ♥Lettuce/Tomato/Onion | ♥WK Corn | ♥Margarine Pat | ♥Italian Pasta Salad | ♥Beverage | ♥Whole Wheat Bread |
| ♥Whole Wheat Bread | ♥Whole Wheat Bread (2) | ♥Whole Wheat Bread | ♥Beverage | ♥Whole Wheat Bread (2) |  | ♥Margarine Pat |
| ♥Margarine Pat | ♥Margarine Pat | ♥Margarine Pat |  | ♥Margarine Pat |  | ♥Beverage |
| ♥Beverage | ♥Beverage | ♥Beverage |  | ♥Beverage |  |  |

## Week 2

### Lunch & Dinner

| Sunday Lunch | Monday Lunch | Tuesday Lunch | Wednesday Lunch | Thursday Lunch | Friday Lunch | Saturday Lunch |
|---|---|---|---|---|---|---|
| ♥Boiled Eggs (2) | ♥Cream of Broccoli Soup | #Cheese Pizza | ♥Hamburger | Fried Chicken | ♥Baked Fish | ♥Sloppy Joe |
| Baked Turkey Ham | ♥Chicken Wrap or | ♥or Cottage Cheese | #or Soy Burger | ♥or Baked Chicken | #or PB & Jelly Sand (2) | #or Soy Sloppy Joe |
| Pancakes | #Hummus Wrap | ♥Spag w/Marinara | French Fries or | #or PB & Jelly Sand (2) | Macaroni & Cheese or | Tater Tots or |
| W/Syrup or | ♥Potato Salad | ♥Garden Salad | ♥Baked Potato | ♥Mashed Potatoes | ♥Garlic Macaroni | ♥Baked Potato |
| ♥Whole Wheat Bread | ♥Green Beans | ♥Ital Dressing Low Cal | ♥Shredded Lettuce | ♥Carrots | ♥Green Beans | ♥Green Peas |
| and ♥Jelly (2) | ♥Margarine Pat | ♥Margarine Pat | ♥Catsup & Mustard | Chicken Gravy | Cornbread or | ♥WW Hamburger Bun |
| ♥Oven Brown Potatoes | ♥Fruit | Dessert or | Pickles | ♥Whole Wheat Bread | ♥Whole Wheat Bread | ♥Margarine Pat |
| ♥Margarine Pat | ♥Beverage | ♥Fruit | Salad Dressing | ♥Margarine Pat | ♥Margarine Pat | Dessert or |
| ♥Fruit | | ♥Beverage | ♥WW Hamburger Bun | Dessert or | Tartar Sauce | ♥Fruit |
| ♥Beverage | | | ♥Margarine Pat | ♥Fruit | ♥Fruit | ♥Beverage |
| | | | ♥Fruit | ♥Beverage | ♥Beverage | |
| | | | ♥Beverage | | | |

| Sunday Dinner | Monday Dinner | Tuesday Dinner | Wednesday Dinner | Thursday Dinner | Friday Dinner | Saturday Dinner |
|---|---|---|---|---|---|---|
| ♥Chili Mac | ♥*Pork Roast | Beef & Bean Burrito or | ♥Old Fashn Bean Soup | ♥Cream of Potato Soup | ♥Turkey Burger | ♥Chicken Tacos |
| #or Soy Chili Mac | #or BBQ Tofu | ♥Bean & Cheese Burrito | Deli Sandwich | Chef Salad | #or Soy Burger | #or Soy Tacos |
| ♥Green Beans | ♥Baked Sweet Potato | Mexican Rice or | #or Hummus | #or Tofu Chef Salad | Sliced Cheese | ♥Cilantro Rice |
| ♥Garden Salad | ♥Peas & Carrots | ♥Steamed Rice | ♥Potato Salad | ♥Beets | Potato Chips or | ♥Pinto Beans |
| ♥Ital Dressing Low Cal | ♥Black Eyed Peas | ♥WK Corn | ♥Lettuce/Onion | ♥Ital Dressing Low Cal | ♥Baked Potato | ♥WK Corn |
| Cornbread or | Barbeque Sauce | Salsa | ♥Mustard | ♥Whole Wheat Bread | ♥Garden Salad | ♥Shredded Lettuce |
| ♥Whole Wheat Bread | ♥Whole Wheat Bread | ♥Margarine Pat | Salad Dressing | ♥Margarine Pat | ♥Ital Dressing Low Cal | ♥Taco Shells (2) |
| ♥Margarine Pat | ♥Margarine Pat | ♥Beverage | ♥WW Hamburger Bun | ♥Beverage | ♥Catsup & Mustard | Salsa |
| ♥Beverage | ♥Beverage | | ♥Margarine Pat | | Salad Dressing | ♥Margarine Pat |
| | | | ♥Beverage | | ♥WW Hamburger Bun | ♥Beverage |
| | | | | | ♥Margarine Pat | |
| | | | | | ♥Beverage | |

* Indicates Pork, # Indicates No Flesh Entree Item, ♥ Indicates Heart Healthy.

## Week 3

### Lunch & Dinner

| Sunday Lunch | Monday Lunch | Tuesday Lunch | Wednesday Lunch | Thursday Lunch | Friday Lunch | Saturday Lunch |
|---|---|---|---|---|---|---|
| Cheese Omelet or | ♥Vegetable Soup | Chicken Patty Sandwich | ♥Hamburger | BBQ Chicken | Breaded Fish Sand or | Ckn Cheese Steak or |
| ♥Plain Omelet | ♥Tuna Salad | ♥or Soy Chicken Patty | #or Soy Burger | ♥or Baked Chicken | ♥Baked Fish | ♥Chicken Salad |
| ♥Oven Brown Potatoes | #or Cheese Sand w/ | ♥Potato Salad | Sliced Cheese | #or Cottage Cheese | #or Soy Burger w/ | #or Cheese Sand w/ |
| Cream Gravy | Salad Dressing | ♥Pinto Beans | Turkey Bacon (2) | ♥Potato Salad | Salad Dressing | Salad Dressing |
| Biscuits (2) or | ♥Lettuce Leaf | ♥Lettuce/Tomato/Onion | Potato Chips or | ♥Carrots | ♥Steamed Rice | ♥Italian Pasta Salad |
| ♥Whole Wheat Bread | ♥Italian Pasta Salad | Salad Dressing | ♥Baked Potato | ♥Whole Wheat Bread | ♥Green Peas | ♥Carrots |
| and ♥Jelly (2) | ♥Whole Wheat Bread (2) | WW Hamburger Bun | ♥Shredded Lettuce | ♥Margarine Pat | ♥Coleslaw | WW Hot Dog Bun |
| ♥Margarine Pat | ♥Margarine Pat | Dessert or | ♥Catsup & Mustard | Dessert or | WW Hamburger Bun | ♥Margarine Pat |
| ♥Fruit | ♥Fruit | ♥Fruit | Pickles | ♥Fruit | ♥Margarine Pat | Dessert or |
| ♥Beverage | ♥Beverage | ♥Margarine Pat | Salad Dressing | ♥Beverage | Tartar Sauce | ♥Fruit |
| | | ♥Beverage | WW Hamburger Bun | | ♥Fruit | ♥Beverage |
| | | | ♥Margarine Pat | | ♥Beverage | |
| | | | ♥Fruit | | | |
| | | | ♥Beverage | | | |

| Sunday Dinner | Monday Dinner | Tuesday Dinner | Wednesday Dinner | Thursday Dinner | Friday Dinner | Saturday Dinner |
|---|---|---|---|---|---|---|
| Chicken Spaghetti or | ♥Chili | ♥Pepper Steak | ♥Black Bean Soup | ♥Roast Beef | ♥Chicken Fajitas | Baked Ziti |
| ♥Chicken & Noodles | #or Soy Chili | #or Tofu Stir Fry | ♥Beef Taco Salad or | #or PB & Jelly Sand (2) | #or Cheese Quesadilla | ♥or Ziti & Beef |
| #or Soy Ckn & Veg | ♥Baked Potato | ♥Steamed Rice | #Soy Taco Salad | ♥Baked Sweet Potato | ♥Cilantro Rice | #or Soy Baked Ziti |
| ♥Green Beans | ♥Diced Onions & Peppers | ♥Steamed Broccoli | Salsa | ♥Simmered Cabbage | ♥Black Beans | ♥Spinach |
| ♥Whole Wheat Bread | Shredded Cheese | ♥Whole Wheat Bread | ♥Whole Wheat Bread | Brown Gravy | ♥Mixed Vegetables | ♥Garden Salad |
| ♥Margarine Pat | ♥WK Corn | ♥Margarine Pat | ♥Margarine Pat | ♥Whole Wheat Bread | Salsa | ♥Ital Dressing Low Cal |
| ♥Beverage | Cornbread or | ♥Beverage | ♥Beverage | ♥Margarine Pat | ♥Flour Tortilla (2) | ♥Whole Wheat Bread |
| | ♥Whole Wheat Bread | | | ♥Beverage | ♥Margarine Pat | ♥Margarine Pat |
| | ♥Margarine Pat | | | | ♥Beverage | ♥Beverage |
| | ♥Beverage | | | | | |

* Indicates Pork, # Indicates No Flesh Entree Item, ♥ Indicates Heart Healthy.

## Week 4

### Lunch & Dinner

| Sunday Lunch | Monday Lunch | Tuesday Lunch | Wednesday Lunch | Thursday Lunch | Friday Lunch | Saturday Lunch |
|---|---|---|---|---|---|---|
| ▼Scrambled Eggs | #Cheese Pizza | Chicken Patty Sandwich | ▼Hamburger | Fried Chicken | ▼Vegetable Soup | ▼Lentil Vegetable Soup |
| Baked Turkey Ham | ▼or Cottage Cheese | ▼for Soy Chicken Patty | ▼or Soy Burger | ▼or Baked Chicken | ▼Tuna Salad | Deli Sandwich |
| French Toast (2) | ▼Spag w/Marinara | ▼Potato Salad | Sliced Cheese | ▼or Cottage Cheese | ▼or Cheese Sand w/ | ▼W or Hummus |
| W/Syrup or | ▼Garden Salad | ▼Pinto Beans | Turkey Bacon (2) | ▼Baked Sweet Potato | Salad Dressing | ▼Potato Salad |
| ▼Whole Wheat Bread | ▼Ital Dressing Low Cal | ▼Lettuce/Tomato/Onion | Potato Chips or | ▼Carrots | ▼Lettuce Leaf | ▼Lettuce/Onion |
| and ▼Jelly (2) | ▼Margarine Pat | Salad Dressing | ▼Baked Potato | ▼Garden Salad | ▼Italian Pasta Salad | ▼Mixed Vegetables |
| ▼Oven Brown Potatoes | ▼Fruit | ▼WW Hamburger Bun | ▼Shredded Lettuce | ▼Ital Dressing Low Cal | ▼WW Hamburger Bun | ▼WW Hamburger Bun |
| ▼Margarine Pat | ▼Beverage | ▼Margarine Pat | ▼Catsup & Mustard | ▼Whole Wheat Bread | ▼Margarine Pat | Salad Dressing |
| ▼Fruit | | Dessert or | Pickles | ▼Margarine Pat | ▼Fruit | ▼Margarine Pat |
| ▼Beverage | | ▼Fruit | Salad Dressing | Dessert or | ▼Beverage | Dessert or |
| | | ▼Beverage | ▼WW Hamburger Bun | ▼Fruit | | ▼Fruit |
| | | | ▼Margarine Pat | ▼Beverage | | ▼Beverage |
| | | | ▼Fruit | | | |
| | | | ▼Beverage | | | |

| Sunday Dinner | Monday Dinner | Tuesday Dinner | Wednesday Dinner | Thursday Dinner | Friday Dinner | Saturday Dinner |
|---|---|---|---|---|---|---|
| ▼BBQ Beef | ▼Chicken Fried Rice | ▼*Pork Roast | Hot Dogs (2) | Pancakes | ▼Turkey Burger | ▼Spaghetti |
| ▼or Soy BBQ | ▼or Tofu Fried Rice | ▼or Cottage Cheese | ▼for Soy Burger w/ | W/Syrup | ▼or Soy Burger | ▼w/Meat Sauce |
| ▼Steamed Rice | ▼Black Beans | ▼Baked Sweet Potato | ▼WW Hamburger Bun | ▼Whole Wheat Bread (2) | Sliced Cheese | ▼for Soy Spag Sauce |
| ▼Green Beans | ▼Carrots | ▼Green Beans | Tater Tots or | and ▼Jelly (2) | Potato Chips or | ▼Steamed Broccoli |
| ▼Whole Wheat Bread | ▼Whole Wheat Bread | ▼Whole Wheat Bread | ▼Baked Potato | Peanut Butter | ▼Baked Potato | ▼Garden Salad |
| ▼Margarine Pat | ▼Margarine Pat | ▼Margarine Pat | ▼Coleslaw | Home Fried Potatoes or | ▼Garden Salad | ▼Ital Dressing Low Cal |
| ▼Beverage | ▼Beverage | ▼Beverage | ▼Catsup & Mustard | ▼Oven Brown Potatoes | ▼Ital Dressing Low Cal | Garlic Bread or |
| | | | ▼WW Hot Dog Buns (2) | ▼Margarine Pat | ▼Catsup & Mustard | ▼Whole Wheat Bread |
| | | | ▼Margarine Pat | ▼Beverage | Salad Dressing | ▼Margarine Pat |
| | | | ▼Beverage | | ▼WW Hamburger Bun | ▼Beverage |
| | | | | | ▼Margarine Pat | |
| | | | | | ▼Beverage | |

* Indicates Pork, # Indicates No Flesh Entree Item, ▼ Indicates Heart Healthy.

## Week 5

### Lunch & Dinner

| Sunday Lunch | Monday Lunch | Tuesday Lunch | Wednesday Lunch | Thursday Lunch | Friday Lunch | Saturday Lunch |
|---|---|---|---|---|---|---|
| ♥Boiled Eggs (2) | Chili Cheese Fries or | Chicken Parmesan or | ♥Hamburger | ♥Baked Chicken | Breaded Fish Sand or | ♥Sloppy Joe |
| French Toast (2) | ♥Soy Chili | ♥Braised Chicken | #or Soy Burger | #or Cottage Cheese | ♥Baked Fish | #or Soy Sloppy Joe |
| W/Syrup or | ♥w/Baked Potato | #or Soy Ckn Chunks | French Fries or | ♥Baked Sweet Potato | #or Cheese Sandwich w/ | Tater Tots or |
| ♥Whole Wheat Bread | ♥Carrots | ♥Spag w/Marinara | ♥Baked Potato | ♥Black Beans | Salad Dressing | ♥Baked Potato |
| and ♥Jelly (2) | ♥Whole Wheat Bread | ♥Spinach | ♥Shredded Lettuce | ♥Spinach | ♥Collard Greens | ♥Green Peas |
| ♥Oven Brown Potatoes | ♥Margarine Pat | Garlic Bread or | ♥Catsup & Mustard | ♥Whole Wheat Bread | ♥Coleslaw | ♥WW Hamburger Bun |
| ♥Margarine Pat | ♥Fruit | ♥Whole Wheat Bread | Pickles | ♥Margarine Pat | ♥WW Hamburger Bun | ♥Margarine Pat |
| ♥Fruit | ♥Beverage | ♥Margarine Pat | Salad Dressing | Dessert or | ♥Margarine Pat | Dessert or |
| ♥Beverage | | Dessert or | ♥WW Hamburger Bun | ♥Fruit | Tartar Sauce | ♥Fruit |
| | | ♥Fruit | ♥Margarine Pat | ♥Beverage | ♥Fruit | ♥Beverage |
| | | ♥Beverage | ♥Fruit | | ♥Beverage | |
| | | | ♥Beverage | | | |

| Sunday Dinner | Monday Dinner | Tuesday Dinner | Wednesday Dinner | Thursday Dinner | Friday Dinner | Saturday Dinner |
|---|---|---|---|---|---|---|
| ♥Beef Tacos | ♥Pepper Steak | *Pork Roast | ♥Old Fashn Bean Soup | Steak & Cheese Sub or | Baked Ziti | ♥Chicken Fajitas |
| #or Soy Tacos | #or Tofu Stir Fry | #or Cottage Cheese | Chef Salad | ♥Roast Beef | ♥or Ziti & Beef | #or Cheese Quesadilla |
| Mexican Rice or | ♥Steamed Rice | ♥Steamed Rice | #or Tofu Chef Salad | #or Soy Burger w/ | #or Soy Baked Ziti | ♥Cilantro Rice |
| ♥Steamed Rice | ♥Steamed Broccoli | ♥Black Beans | ♥Beets | Salad Dressing | ♥Spinach | ♥Pinto Beans |
| ♥Black Beans | ♥Whole Wheat Bread | ♥Mixed Vegetables | ♥Ital Dressing Low Cal | Potato Chips or | ♥Garden Salad | ♥WK Corn |
| ♥WK Corn | ♥Margarine Pat | ♥Whole Wheat Bread | ♥Whole Wheat Bread (2) | ♥Baked Potato | ♥Ital Dressing Low Cal | Salsa |
| Salsa | ♥Beverage | ♥Margarine Pat | ♥Margarine Pat | ♥Green Beans | ♥Whole Wheat Bread | ♥Flour Tortilla (2) |
| ♥Taco Shells (2) | | ♥Beverage | ♥Beverage | ♥WW Hot Dog Bun | ♥Margarine Pat | ♥Margarine Pat |
| ♥Margarine Pat | | | | ♥Margarine Pat | ♥Beverage | ♥Beverage |
| ♥Beverage | | | | ♥Beverage | | |

\* Indicates Pork, # Indicates No Flesh Entree Item, ♥ Indicates Heart Healthy.

## REGULATION AND ENFORCEMENT

In the United States, regulation is common among governmental agencies, and the standards we have for other food facilities are quite clear (sometimes too strict, sometimes not enough, but always surely in place). I wondered whether the policing of foodservice operations in correctional facilities would be the responsibility of the US Department of Agriculture (USDA) to create the guidelines, or maybe the Food and Drug Administration (FDA) had a hand in things, or perhaps Health and Human Services, or County Health Inspectors came often to frisk the joints. One would certainly think that such things as nutritional standards, cooking conditions, and sanitation rules would be handed down from on high with strict enforcement that they were being carried out and that safe food preparation conditions were in practice at correctional facilities. The reality is that none of that is the case.

The US government prides itself with the rigor of inspection our food goes through, and a myriad of laws keep the safety of our food in check, not only ensuring decent quality, but also ensuring that it is well-produced and sanitary. Health inspections, heavy regulation, and an enormous number of rules have been created over the years to keep food-producing and -serving facilities in tight check to protect public health. Whereas, for much of the late nineteenth and twentieth centuries, food law became more and more heavily regulated with the creation of governmental departments and regulatory agencies dedicated to the cause, prison law (and prison food law specifically) went increasingly overlooked and has remained as such. And, whereas general food law in the United States derives from consumer demand and a capital-driven system, prisoners lack the clout and voice to impact change.

Food law for regular citizens differs completely from that for prisoners. Rather than hold to the standards with which regular food is regulated, state legislatures have, according to Cyrus Naim of Harvard Law School, "adopted a laissez-faire approach" to prison food regulation, "leaving wardens to run their prisons as they see fit. It is prison administrators who decide what to serve inmates, how often, and whether they will choose to run their own inspections at all."[8] While the state or other semiregulatory agencies will make suggestions about how to properly run facilities (and the FDA publishes numerous guides on how to maintain safe facilities), generate handbooks, and attempt to *influence* how correctional institutions run their kitchens, there is no governmental agency dedicated to oversight and enforcement of correctional facility foodservices. Correctional institutions in America are not overseen by public health officials. That is to say, correctional facilities conduct their own inspections of their own foodservice facilities: "In the absence of outside oversight, much of prison regulation is done from within. That is, prisons themselves will often voluntarily attempt to set and comply with standards they or others create."[9] Any major changes to the way correctional facilities run their foodservice is through legal means when a prisoner is somehow able to make a legal case, generally using the Eighth Amendment to say that their constitutional rights are being violated. One can imagine how rarely this goes through (more on that in chapter 5).

Generally, correctional facilities check themselves against "industry standards" and have either state- or facility-specific handbooks for regulation. And, of course, the food that enters these facilities comes from corporations and factories following governmental regulations. However:

> there can be no revocation of licenses because state funded prisons obviously are not *given* licenses. They cannot be. When a restaurant fails inspection, and its license is revoked, it may simply be closed down. There are plenty of other restaurants consumers may go to, and, with the exception of the restaurant owner and staff, no one who will be seriously harmed. The same is not true of a prison kitchen. Inmates have to eat, whether the kitchen that provides their food is sanitary or not. It cannot be shut down because there is no other source from which inmates can get their food.[10]

Again, the lack of public outrage surrounding conditions comes into play here: Prisoners' voices, purposefully suppressed, are not loud enough to cause the public outcry needed to enact change. And, even if word got out about abominable conditions, public opinion of prisoners is so low, one wonders who would feel compelled to cry out on their behalf.

A couple of exceptions could be noted. One is that correctional facilities can enroll in a certification program of sorts with the American Correctional Association (ACA) that has claimed to come up with a set of best practices surrounding facility operation.[11] Once completed, the facility is "accredited" by the ACA, but the benefits seem to be oriented toward the business side of corrections, such as being less likely to get sued, reducing liability, and streamlining costs. According to their Web site, "Accredited agencies have a stronger defense against litigation through documentation and the demonstration of a 'good faith' effort to improve conditions of confinement."[12] The other is that some states have governmental departments to keep an eye on corrections, such as in Rhode Island where a general law applying to all facilities that prepare food does cover corrections, but generally comes into use when an outbreak or issue occurs—not for general, consistent inspection and regulation of correctional facilities.[13] California has the California Government Office of the Inspector General, whose mission, according to their Web site, is to "assist in safeguarding the integrity of the State's correctional system—in effect, to act as the eyes and ears of the public in overseeing the State's prisons and correctional programs."[14] That being said, it does not seem to have much of a role in overseeing food. Perusing their annual reports shows that foodservice does not fall under their purview, leaving me to believe that, as in many other states, that aspect of things is self-monitored from correctional facility to correctional facility.

In sum, regulation of prison food is uncoordinated and minimal at best:

> Since the legislatures have been unwilling to legislate minimum standards, those standards come instead either from within, through self-regulation, or through the courts, which outline the limits on prisoner treatment mandated by various constitutional amendments. The result is a two sizes fit all approach. In the first case, there is no real enforcement, just goodwill. In the second, enforcement is both haphazard and often unwieldy.[15]

## SPECIAL DIETS

It is almost impossible to conceptualize that a group of thousands of people, in any circumstance, could get by with eating the same thing. Inevitably, in every large group circumstance, there are dietary restrictions, allergies, sensitivities, not to mention likes and dislikes. Consider when you book an international airline ticket these days—the scroll down menu of options for your in-flight meal ranges from Halal to dairy-free to vegetarian to "bland meal." Think about the current craze of gluten free, or vegetarianism, veganism, paleo, and so on. Diet-related diseases also necessitate their own avoidances or additives to the usual regimen. So, what happens to these populations when they get sent to prison and how are special diets and food needs accommodated? Are they?

### Being, or Going, Kosher

When my friend was writing me from prison, many things struck me, appalled me, and puzzled me about the tales he had about the food he ate, but one incredible thing stood out: He converted to Judaism in prison in order to simply get more fresh fruits and vegetables from the kosher meal (fruit in prison and jail seems to be a particular rarity, as inmates can smuggle it back to their cells to make prison hooch with it). While this was surprising to me, because it seemed extreme to go to such lengths, as I began to dig into it a trend emerged, complete with a *New York Times* article entitled, "You Don't Have to Be Jewish to Love a Kosher Prison Meal" in which author Lizette Alvarez details the phenomenon in Florida, which in 2014 had been put under court order to begin offering a kosher meal to eligible inmates.[16] At issue was the fact that the kosher meal for these Florida inmates cost, on average, four times more than the typical prison fare, and correctional administrators were concerned that they would see a boom in requests for kosher meals once they rolled it out, which had happened in other states.

The desire for a kosher meal can come from many places, but a distinct rise in prisoners claiming to be (or being) Jewish has accompanied the awareness that with it comes a stand-out meal. One must wonder how appalling the food must be in prison to commit to a new religion, because it is not simply enough to make one declaration, but, at least in my friend's case, he had to continue showing up to Temple and practicing with the other Jewish prisoners in order to continue receiving the special meal. As Alvarez muses, "In a world of few choices, the meals are a novelty, a chance to break from the usual ritual of prison life. Others believe the kosher turkey cutlets and spaghetti and meatballs simply taste better. But some see it as a safer bet [health wise]."[17] Kosher food often comes pre-packaged and is therefore considered uncontaminated and, in addition, trades at a higher commodity value on the prison black market than the typical food smuggled out of the chow hall.[18]

In a 2012 article the Jewish news journal *Forward* reported that, at that time, in federal correctional facilities, there were "4,127 individuals receiving a so-called Certified Religious Diet out of a total of 217,000 inmates, or about 2 percent of the population" and estimated that about one in six of those taking kosher meals are, in fact, Jewish.[19] Since 2000, under the passage of the *Religious Land Use and Institutionalized Persons Act (RLUIPA)*, prisons have been mandated to serve food that meets the dietary requirements of an inmate's religion.[20]

According to another article on the topic of going kosher in prison, published in the journal *Western Folklore*, author Steve Siporin points out his surprise in inmates wanting to claim to be Jewish, given the deep racial and religious segregation that already exists, and notes that historically Jews would generally not self-identify in prison, but "In past times, one of the ways a Jew in prison might be recognized would be by his refusal to eat pork and his attempts to follow the rules of kashrut as well as possible within the prison system, perhaps eating vegetarian."[21] Siporin is also keen to point out that the kosher meal is favored for the belief that, in addition to having more nutrients and fresher ingredients, it also contains more calories, claiming that some have said kosher meals provide up to 5,400 calories per day versus the usual 3,000. To a prisoner, this means being able to bulk up more, and therefore more easily protect oneself.[22]

## Vegans/Vegetarians

What if your right to eat what you believe in is not protected under the Constitution, as religious beliefs are protected? But your moral convictions surrounding a topic are as strong as, if not stronger than, many people's religious ones? This was the case for a man in Mill Valley, California, in 2011. When Dave McDonald was put in jail for ninety-nine days, he refused to eat anything that was not animal-free, and as a result, ended up losing almost fifty pounds.[23] His case, backed by People for the Ethical Treatment of Animals (PETA), raised public interest over how accommodating the state needs to be in making special meals for inmates. Under a strict interpretation of Prop 15 in the state of California, the jail was within its legal rights to only accommodate religious and spiritual beliefs, but in the *New York Times* article about what happened, it seemed that the jail (and many others) already had the ability to make vegetarian meals, so why McDonald was denied is fuzzy.[24] It seems only right to mention that McDonald was later cleared of the original charges brought against him.

The case highlights an overarching theme for vegetarians and vegans who enter the system of corrections: it seems that it really just depends where and when you enter the system. That being said, the Bureau of Prisons Policy Food Service Manual program statement says that a "no-flesh protein option will be provided at both noon and evening meals whenever a main entree containing flesh is offered."[25]

Online forums abound on the topic with tips and tricks for surviving prison as a vegetarian and a list of the "Top 10 Vegetarian Friendly Prisons" is on PETA's Web site (these did not list specific correctional facilities, so they are presented with a bit of skepticism):[26]

1. **Idaho** offers a lentil shepherd's pie, vegan pizza, vegan Mexican pie, soy patties, soy sausage, veggie loaf, veggie lasagna, veggie meatballs, vegan hot cakes, vegan biscuits, cookies, cakes, pies, and puddings.
2. **Massachusetts** offers meatless chicken macaroni casserole, vegetable bologna, veggie burger, veggie meatballs, meatless chicken cutlet, meatless chicken nuggets, vegetable chop suey, vegetarian chicken stew.
3. **Pennsylvania** offers tofu cacciatore, soy BBQ, tofu stir fry, veggie burger, soy Salisbury steak, soy meatballs, tofu scramble, soy croquette, soy sausage patties, soy loaf, soy pasta casserole, soy stuffed cabbage, and soy stew.
4. **Georgia** offers vegan BBQ, meatless deli slices, veggie patty, vegan breakfast patties, vegan chili, baked macaroni crumble, stir fried vegetables and oriental sauce, tofu scramble, vegan cornbread, vegan cookies, vegan cakes, vegan pies, vegan brownies, vegan muffins, and vegan peach cobbler.
5. **New Hampshire** offers chili with texturized vegetable protein, chop suey with texturized vegetable protein, shepherd's pie with texturized vegetable protein, veggie links, lentil meatballs, grilled tofu sandwich, vegetarian pot pie, vegetable stir fry, hummus, vegetable tacos, vegetable chow mein, vegetable stew, and several vegetable soups.
6. **Utah** offers sweet and sour tofu, tofu taco rice casserole, vegetable and tofu chow mein, veggie burgers, veggie dogs, veggie meatballs, tofu a la king, lots of tofu dishes.

7. **Hawaii** offers vegetarian shepherd's pie with texturized vegetable protein, vegetarian stuffed cabbage with texturized vegetable protein, vegetarian stew with texturized vegetable protein, grilled tofu slices, vegetarian teriyaki burger, and vegetarian long rice with tofu.

8. **Tennessee** offers texturized vegetable protein a la king, vegetarian sweet and sour, veggie burger, vegetarian chili, vegetarian stir fry, and texturized vegetable protein country gravy.

9. **Kansas** offers a veggie burger, taco crunch, burrito, meatless pasta, meatless chili, loaded baked potato, vegetable rice soup.

10. **North Dakota** offers a veggie burger, meatless sloppy joes, vegetable fajitas, vegetable noodle stew, vegetable potato soup.

Over at *VICE News*, a "Strict Vegan Prisoner Handbook" which advises vegan inmates to try a battery of tactics, including tapping the commissary for the entirety of your meals, going on a hunger strike to provoke getting what you want, and becoming kosher to get fresh fruits.[27] And a prisoner wrote a short essay on the difficulties of keeping vegan in prison for the compilation book *Fourth City: Essays From the Prison in America* in which he said:

> Adhering to a healthy vegan diet in prison is a complex task. Mashed potatoes are whipped with milk, cornbread contains dairy and eggs, and the only meat alternatives are eggs and cheese, or texturized vegetable protein often covered in sauce laced with whey. I supplement my diet with commissary items like canned beans, tomato paste, pasta, and rice. . . . I order soy products when my 8-cent an hour "job" permits.[28]

## Inmates with Diabetes

According to an article published on *The Marshall Project*, inmates with diabetes are "often at the mercy of prison staff to manage their diabetes" and are not put on a particular diet oriented to the needs of their disease.[29] The article highlights the case of one inmate, Donald Lippert, who suffered multiple seizures and poor treatment of his type-1 diabetes while serving time in a federal correctional facility in Illinois, having even at times been denied insulin when the need for it conflicted with the schedule of the prison regimen. The biggest barrier to self-management seems to be the use of needles, for checking glucose levels and administering the insulin, and even self-regulating insulin pumps (hugely popular among type-1 sufferers these days) can be considered contraband.[30] Both the American Diabetes Association and the Federal Bureau of Prisons have suggested protocols for inmate diabetes management, which generally suggest injection times being close to mealtimes and offering healthier food alternatives.[31]

## CELEBRATORY MEALS AND HOLIDAYS

Whether or not you are incarcerated, the holidays still come around once a year, and when we think about the holidays we think about food—it's part of our culture as Americans. Food is a huge part of the way we celebrate holidays, whether it is Fourth of July barbecues, Easter ham, or Jewish latkes at Hanukkah. In prison, special food is often made to acknowledge the holidays, and for prisoners it is a big deal, something to look forward to in the face of otherwise completely monotonous fare. The BOP Food Service Manual stipulates that holiday meals be prepared special for these occasions, but ingredients may not deviate from the normal certified food list.[32]

The prison holiday tradition has been going on for years, even sometimes involving the public who tend to be more sympathetic to prisoners over the holidays—photos of female volunteers unpacking boxes of special food over Christmas at San Quentin prison recently surfaced and were published on *The Marshall Project.*[33]

Holidays can be opportunities for inmates to break down barriers and eat together over a special meal.

> One important festival preparation at Eastham involved food acquisition. Prior to Christmas, inmates who could afford to bought and packed away food from the prison commissary to consume on Christmas Eve. The commissary was well stocked with special items such as beef sausage, candy, fresh fruit, and fruitcakes. By Christmas Eve the living areas overflowed with luxury foods. Inmates pooled their "goodies" on the dayroom domino tables to make "spreads" for group meals. . . . All three ethnic groups, ordinarily tightly segregated, commingled when eating.[34]

But the holiday meal experience is always varied and not necessarily well-executed, and overall never seems to be quite like what one would get at home. One inmate explained his holiday behind bars:

> We would receive a handful of meals a year which were actually decent. Christmas in Fed Prison meant a Cornish hen. As populations grew over the years that was reduced to half a hen. We got one steak a year on New Year's but it was not edible. Imagine a steak so tough that it could not be chewed. On top of that we only had plastic knives to cut the meat so that meant it could not be cut. We got ribs or BBQ on the 4th, with potato salad. On Easter we would usually get fried chicken breast. Thanksgiving we got a huge turkey leg. There was a common understanding that it was really an emu leg. I don't know for sure but it was so big it took up the entire tray. No exaggeration. It was greasy and nasty. Not really edible but every year we got it.[35]

The "Country's Toughest Sheriff" (self-proclaimed) Joe Arpaio of Arizona (discussed in chapter 3) had cut meat entirely out of his jail menu. He boasted on

Twitter in 2015 that his Thanksgiving Day menu for his inmates cost a mere fifty-six cents per inmate. He captioned it by writing, "Thanksgiving menu is all set! Hope the inmates give thanks for this special meal being served in the jails tomorrow."[36] For National Hotdog Day in July 2015, Arpaio posted to Facebook, saying he'd made an exception for the day to his meatless rule, by serving hotdogs, but only to incarcerated military veterans.

# 5

# Food as Protest, Food as Punishment

The role of food in prison has always been more than just to satiate and placate inmates. In prison, food often equates to power, whether on its own or as currency for inmates. As already shown, food creates a micro-economy within the prison walls due to its pleasure value for prisoners. Food's value is based on two things: the void (or lack of enough) and the lack of choice. Any opportunity to subvert the restrictions imposed upon daily life in prison is an opportunity to connect to feeling the freedoms of being on the outside. More than just rebellious acts, choices of any kind around food re-appropriate selfhood for inmates. As sociologist Rebecca Godderis wrote:

> the "taken for granted," everyday act of defining one's self through the consumption of food becomes a highly charged issue in prison where the sense of one's personal identity is transformed. Inside of prison, a person is an inmate, not an individual. Therefore, because food is such a central part of the daily prison routine and because it acts as such a powerful symbol of identity, the consumption of food is an excellent means to express power in prison.[1]

Food's power is twofold: It holds sway over prisoners as the metronomic device of the day and often the only source of pleasure, but it also becomes a tool for inmates to utilize in challenging guards or fellow inmates. This chapter delves into the ways in which food, as a powerful force, can shape and change conditions inside the prison walls. "Eating the official food . . . is somewhat like eating the entire prison, like making the prison part of you. On the other hand, throwing the horrible food away and making your own amounts to fighting for dignity and sense of self."[2]

## CHALLENGING CONDITIONS: THE EIGHTH AMENDMENT

As discussed in chapter 4, prison food kitchens are self-inspected and self-regulated entities, so challenging the quality, safety, and security of the food prepared in them is often incredibly difficult for inmates. After being convicted of a crime and sentenced to prison, what rights does a prisoner have? As we know, certainly not the same as those of a regular citizen, but also certainly not none at all. While every correctional facility has a method and protocol by which inmates can lodge complaints, even formal ones, these often go unheeded. Perhaps just making the complaint and feeling that it was read can make inmates feel better about what they think has wronged them, but on a humanitarian level, there is little regulation or formality of process surrounding these complaints, even if they are grave.

The means by which correctional facilities are regulated ensures that the way conditions actually can be changed for inmates from the bottom up is through the sole use of lawsuits. And these lawsuits, usually self-filed, rarely go anywhere. If, somehow, an inmate is able to afford and file the proper paperwork, from their cell, to pursue a lawful claim against the facility in which they are housed, it is no guarantee that they will be given a hearing: "Whether a prisoner's claim proceeds beyond the complaint stage depends largely on the attitude with which the magistrate or district judge views the complaint. . . . Estimates of the percentage of successful inmate suits vary from 6 percent to 13 percent. This is far below even other types of cases known for low success rates."[3]

This is perhaps because a prisoner must file a lawsuit that challenges not just local or state jurisdiction, but the Constitution of the United States under the Eighth Amendment. Yes, in order to win (or even be able to challenge) their case, a prisoner's only line of argument is to contend that their Eighth Amendment right, as stated in the Constitution of the United States, is being violated. The Eighth Amendment includes a clause called "The Cruel and Unusual Punishment Clause," which *Legal Dictionary* says "restricts the severity of punishments that state and federal governments may impose upon persons who have been convicted of criminal offense."[4]

"Cruel and unusual punishment" means not only physical assault and torture, but can also include mental aggression against inmates. Of course, entire books (fascinating ones, even) have been written about the Eighth Amendment and its use for and against prisoners in the penal system in America. What is important to note for our purposes is, again, that, in order for food conditions to be truly changed, a prisoner would need to bring a lawsuit against their institution using the Eighth Amendment argument, insinuating that the meals they are being served are inhumane, and their counsel would need to prove that the inmate(s) is (are) suffering a form of cruel and unusual punishment. Prisoners do not have many true rights beyond the use of this part of our national legal backbone, and therefore, it is, not surprisingly, intensely difficult to effect change.

> For millennia, the basic rules of punishment went unquestioned. To the extent confinement was used it was completely unregulated. Yet by the late eighteenth century, some of the same factors at work in food law seemed to come to the fore [for prisons]. . . . Unfortunately, the comparison seems to end there. Rather than continuing to follow a pattern of constant improvement and growth of the law, it instead followed a consistent downward slope. First it moved into a rut where occasionally there was talk of reform, but no real changes ever manifested.

As noted in chapter 4, self-regulation is truly the name of the game for correctional facilities.

## Lawsuits

While most inmate grievances and efforts to challenge the system have fallen on deaf ears due to lack of legal knowledge or judges simply throwing them out, a few cases have actually made waves in attempting to change the status quo when it comes to prison food. A paper put forth by the organization Americans for Effective Law Enforcement (AELE) in 2007 notes many of the most significant cases—ones that have shaped foodways in prison. Regarding general conditions for prisoners, the question is always between the public's perception of "comfort" and "luxury" versus the necessity and right of prisoners to have their needs met. The paper articulates the cases that have shaped general regulations:

> General standards for when conditions of confinement violate constitutional rights were set by *Bell v. Wolfish*, 441 U.S. 520 (1979), and *Rhodes v. Chapman*, 452 U.S. 337 (1981), and subsequently further developed and clarified by *Wilson v. Seiter*, 504 U.S. 294 (1991). Rhodes indicates that prisoners are not entitled to luxury or "comfort" in prisons and jails, but that the running of those facilities must be conducted in a manner "compatible with the evolving standards of decency that mark the progress of a maturing society."[5]

More often than changing the system, cases from inmates contesting the Eighth Amendment are rejected by the courts. A 2006 case, *Freeman v. Berge*, No. 05-2820, U.S. Appl. Lexis 7149 (7th Cir.) in which a prisoner was suing for having lost forty-five pounds during a 2½ year period, was dismissed when the court found out that he was refusing to obey prison rules when receiving his meals.[6] Prisons will often require inmates to stand in line or in a certain place in their cell when receiving meals. Failure to obey can result in denial of meals. According to the AELE paper:

> The prisoner, on many occasions, refused to put on pants or gym shorts, insisting on eating in his underwear, and therefore was refused a number of meals. The facility also refused to serve him when he had a sock on his head, which might be used as a weapon, depending on what was in it, when he was asleep, or when his cell walls were smeared with blood and feces that he refused to clean up. The court also noted that the weight loss was not detrimental to his health, and he actually ended up "closer to the normal weight for a person of his height" at the end of the time period than he had been at the beginning.[7]

A myriad of other lawsuits highlight the unsuccessful attempts by prisoners to change their conditions, despite such things as mice or bugs found in food (*Black-well v. Patten*), denial of hot meals to prisoners (*Cosby v. Purkett* and *Amos v. Simmons*), and the serving of two meals a day instead of three (*White v. Gregory* and *Gardner v. Beale*).[8]

In 2009, an injunction attempt was denied by a judge in Colorado when Oklahoma City Bombing coconspirator Terry L. Nichols brought the case against his prison, claiming that it was serving unhealthy, refined foods and that he needed more whole grains and fresh food.[9] The judge ruled that Nichols did not face "immediate and irreparable injury" due to his diet.[10]

## Hunger Strikes in Prison

Hunger strikes in prison are perhaps as old as prisons themselves. In thinking through the ways in which prisoners can peacefully rail against their plight, it is not hard to understand why a hunger strike is a particularly effective and powerful solution. It is the obligation of the state to keep the prisoner alive and at least minimally nourished. As stated earlier, food is a powerful tool in coercion within prison, and the hunger strike is an excellent paradigm of that.

In 1917, the famous American Suffragist Alice Paul was sent to jail for seven months for picketing at the White House. After less than a month in a Washington jail, she joined with six other women to go on hunger strike, protesting specifically the food.[11] In the *New York Times* article about the incident, the paper said, "she had been in the jail hospital without food for the preceding twenty-four hours, stolidly threatening to starve herself to death unless her six companions, serving time for the same offense, got better food."[12] The article also notes that this was not her first hunger strike, having performed a similar act in an English jail some years prior. The *New York Times* calls her a "slight, little woman, weighing about ninety pounds and of delicate constitution" and that the diet she and her fellow compatriots had been offered consisted "principally of salt pork and cabbage at the rate of eighteen times in thirteen days."[13] This, in turn, gained national attention and the group came to use the events to leverage even more attention to their Suffragist cause. Eventually, Paul was force-fed and put into a psychiatric ward for evaluation, but she never wavered in her convictions. Under new and growing sympathy from the public, Paul was eventually released and able to continue fighting for the cause of suffrage—a conviction many believed she had shown she was willing to die fighting for.[14]

In 1972, Judith Ward was incarcerated in Great Britain at the age of twenty-five, accused of bombing a bus that killed twelve people. In prison for eighteen years, only to have her innocence later proven, she has described in detail many aspects of the experience of the conditions of incarceration. At one point, she describes a passionate hunger strike:

> On the day in question, twenty-six women refused their meals. The press, already alerted, phoned the wing for details and so we began a protest which called for conditions to be modernized and even for the closing of the wing on psychological grounds. . . . It wasn't a hunger strike in the sense that we were prepared to starve to death (although we didn't let authorities know this), it was an attempt to better general conditions.[15]

John Lennon's killer, Mark David Chapman, was transferred to a psychiatric unit after he began a hunger strike and expressed his intention to take his life by starvation. The prison, after seeking a court order to do so, ended up force feeding him.[16] Chapman is currently still alive and in prison in upstate New York.

## 2013 California Prisons Hunger Strike

Hunger strikes are not always simply over the food, but are effective, powerful modes of peaceful protest.

Recent history has shown the power of the prison hunger strike. What may have been the largest hunger strike in history started at the Pelican Bay State Prison. Pelican Bay is a supermax prison that holds a total of 3,500 prisoners with 1,500 in solitary confinement (that is almost 35 percent of the entire population). The prisoners have been subjected to intense punishment: being sent to Secure Housing Units (SHUs), also known as "the hole" or solitary confinement, for any number of reasons that can be attributed to "gang affiliation," including creating a Christmas card with stars on it (thought to be gang symbols).[17] Public perception of solitary confinement is that it is a generally temporary punishment, where inmates go for a

week as a result of bad behavior, but the reality is that tens of thousands of prisoners across the United States spend years in extreme isolation, with Pelican Bay being a particularly acute example. According to *Mother Jones*, which listed Pelican
Bay State Prison as one of the ten worst prisons in America in 2013, the conditions
for prisoners in the SHU are particularly bleak and isolating:

> At Pelican Bay, the state's first and most notorious supermax, the 1,500 occupants of
> the Security Housing Unit (SHU) and Administrative Housing Unit spend 22.5 hours a
> day alone in windowless cells measuring about 7 x 11 feet. The remaining ninety min-
> utes are spent, also alone, in bare concrete exercise pens. With no phone calls allowed,
> and only the rare non-contact visit, these prisoners, like those at ADX and Texas' Allan
> Polunsky Unit, can only access the world outside their cells via their "feeding slots."
> And their only interactions with fellow prisoners consists of shouting through steel
> mesh—until the guards ordered them to shut up.[18]

In addition, inmates determined to be gang members at Pelican Bay are sent
to solitary confinement and remain there indefinitely, with their potential release
from the SHU being reviewed only once every six years.[19] In protest against this
treatment, nearly thirty thousand inmates from two-thirds of the prisons in California began refusing meals in July 2013.[20] This was after a smaller, but also well-
organized hunger strike in 2011. While the 2013 protest was mainly centered on
California's "aggressive solitary confinement practices," it turned quickly into a
prisoner- and public-supported cause that demanded improved prison conditions
across the system of corrections. A *New York Magazine* article about the Pelican
Bay hunger strike outlines how four inmates, all isolated in SHUs, were able to co-
ordinate the strike. The main instigator of the strike, an inmate named Todd Ashker,
had been in solitary confinement in an SHU for almost twenty-five years. He told
*New York Magazine* reporter Benjamin Wallace-Wells, "I have not had a normal
face-to-face conversation with another human being in twenty-three years."[21] To
be clear, Ashker is an inmate with a track record of intense violence, a member of
the Aryan Brotherhood, and is in the SHU for stabbing to death another inmate. He
refers to his own life as a "waste of space" in his interview with Wallace-Wells.[22]
That being said, many of the accounts of the use of SHUs question whether or not
intense solitary isolation and the complete loss of social connection contribute to
or detract from heinous behavior, with one thing being certain: the SHUs are on
the edge of cruel and unusual punishment, simply given their intense psychological
effects: making prisoners socially inept.

Inspired by the protesting acts of British political figure and hunger striker
Bobby Sands, and the revolutionary texts of writers such as Michel Foucault,
Howard Zinn, and Naomi Wolf, Ashker and other gang leaders banded together
in their cell block, shouting through toilet pipes and across concrete walls to

plant the seed for the hunger strike.[23] According to Wallace-Wells's report in his interview with Ashker, a hunger strike was decided on over many months of cross-pod conversations through thick walls and using various codes and slang. The same men who were originally dedicated to tearing each other apart as members of rival gangs were now aligning themselves against the bigger apparatus of prison injustice:

> The men planned for the hunger strike meticulously. They had staged two more modest strikes in 2011, and afterward some had staged private fasts in their cells to try to learn how long they might be able to go without food. The four men had spent the spring putting on weight. Ashker had calculated how much water he needed to drink to keep his electrolytes balanced, his heart pumping: 240 ounces a day. In June, the men sent letters to an activist group detailing their grievances, explaining when the strike would begin, and asking other prisoners to join them. In letters to families and friends, they spread the word. Corrections officers throughout the state heard the news; on July 2, [2014] a few senior officials visited from Sacramento to meet with the prisoners and measure their intent. They left convinced the men were serious. Then, a few days later, the prisoners stopped eating.[24]

According to many articles written about the Pelican Bay hunger strike, no one could have anticipated its extent and depth, in which tens of thousands of prisoners across the state began to forgo eating. Not only does this speak to the powerful nature in which inmates communicate within and across prisons, it also begs the understanding of how deeply needed these prison reforms are, according to inmates. While many lasted only a few days, slowly, the movement began to see public support as protests of support were staged in Los Angeles and Berkeley, California. Celebrities Bonnie Raitt and Jay Leno wrote letters of support.[25] Some of the leaders held out for the entire summer, lasting almost sixty days without food, certainly pushing the edge of death in exchange for free expression.[26]

When a judge ordered force-feeding of the prisoners that had held out, including Ashker and other gang leaders, they decided to end the strike. But the seed was planted, and in September of 2015, Ashker, in conjunction with the Center for Constitutional Rights, won a lawsuit against the state of California.[27] In *Ashker vs. Brown* (State of California), two major victories in reform have been ordered for solitary confinement:

1. The settlement transforms California's use of solitary confinement from a status-based system to a behavior-based system.
2. Validated gang affiliates who are found guilty of an SHU-eligible offense will enter a quicker two-year SHU step-down program for return to general population after serving their determinate SHU term.[28]

Most importantly, this means the abolition of indefinite sentences to solitary confinement, and prisoners who have been "gang validated" will be sent to a two-year, four-step program after serving their SHU sentence.[29] In terms of corrections and the stodginess of the system, this is a momentous victory with relatively sweeping reforms. It should be noted that Ashker obtained a paralegal certificate through a correspondence course in his time spent in the SHU, and has since seemingly made it his hobby and mission to challenge the system and push for reform. The success that he has seen over the years since the hunger strikes has shown its huge impact on bringing about change.

## FOOD AS PUNISHMENT: NUTRALOAF

It's possible that you may have come across an article about a notorious and nefarious (and technically nutritious) prison food item called nutraloaf (or nutriloaf, it has been spelled both ways). Also known as "discipline loaf," "food loaf," "management meal," or simply "the loaf," nutraloaf is more than food—it is a tool. When we talk about prison and its food on the spectrum from pleasure to punishment, nutraloaf falls quite clearly at the punishment end. It is, in fact, solely given out to misbehaving prisoners. Where we traditionally conceptualize flavorless bread and water being fed to inmates who have been misbehaving, as an NPR article stated, "the loaf is . . . a bland, brownish lump . . . rendered even more unappetizing by being served in a small paper sack, with no seasoning."[30] So, what is it and how is it used for punishment?

Nutraloaf is, in a way, exactly what it sounds like: a loaf of *something* mashed up and baked up to be nothing but a vehicle for nutrients for an inmate. The idea is that the foodservice providers generally take whatever is left over from the day's meal, blend it together and bake it into one tasteless, loathsome loaf intended simply to meet a nutrition quota. It is specifically intended to be void of flavor, and therefore any notion of pleasure. One "recipe" obtained by *Mother Jones* in a court brief from the Vermont appellate court said that the nutraloaf in their corrections system contained: "whole wheat bread, non-dairy cheese, raw carrots, spinach, seedless raisins, Great Northern beans, vegetable oil, tomato paste, powdered milk, and dehydrated potato flakes" and that "these ingredients are 'mixed and baked.'"[31] The sense from reading descriptions of nutraloaf, however, is that there is no specific recipe and often the mixture hinges on what is left lying around at the end of the day or week. Another description of the "recipe" is described as follows: "Nutraloaf contains everything from carrots and cabbage to kidney beans and potatoes, plus shadowy ingredients such as "dairy blend" and "mechanically separated poultry." You purée everything into a paste, shape it into a loaf, and bake it for 50 to 70 minutes at 375 degrees."[32]

Inmate Aaron Fraser, serving time between 2004 and 2007, was "given the loaf" described to NPR, "They take a bunch of guck, like whatever they have available, and they put it in some machine." Fraser says, "I would have to be on the point of dizziness when I know I have no choice [to eat it]."[33] While it may not seem to be that awful in description, the deprivation of taste becomes pretty punishing, because nutraloaf is not given once to an inmate, but is fed to him or her repeatedly over the course of a number of days or weeks.

When *Chicago* magazine food critic Jeff Ruby sampled the loaf at Cook County Jail (served by Aramark), he decided it constituted writing an article dedicated to describing its blandness:

> The mushy, disturbingly uniform innards recalled the thick, pulpy aftermath of something you dissected in biology class: so intrinsically disagreeable that my throat nearly closed up reflexively. But the funny thing about Nutraloaf is the taste. It's not awful, nor is it especially good. I kept trying to detect any individual element—carrot? egg?—and failing. Nutraloaf tastes blank, as though someone physically removed all hints of flavor.[34]

Nutraloaf has danced around legality and ended up skirting, but toeing the line of the Eighth Amendment. According to the NPR article, twenty-two cases have been brought to the courts against nutraloaf, and none of them have succeeded, thus allowing its ambiguous use in corrections to continue.[35] While it is estimated that around one hundred institutions use "the loaf," there is no clear data on who, where, and how it is used including punishment protocols.[36] Issues and lawsuits have been consistently raised surrounding whether or not use of nutraloaf constitutes cruel and unusual punishment, not solely because of its blandness, but accounts of it making prisoners ill and sick have also surfaced: An inmate named Terrance Prude in Milwaukee, in a *Time* article about nutraloaf, said that he had a horrible reaction to the loaf, losing almost ten pounds in just a matter of days while also suffering from stomach pain, vomiting, and anal fissures.[37] In a lawsuit filed shortly thereafter, Prude won a five-figure settlement after a judge concluded that he had been harmed and after the company running the foodservice initially refused to hand over the recipe they used.

While nutraloaf technically feeds prisoners the minimum amount of nutrients and calories for the day, the question of deprivation still certainly remains: How much can we deprive people based on how much of an offense? While technically, "there's no guidance from the government on using the loaf . . . the American Correctional Association, which accredits prisons and sets best practices for the industry, discourages using food as a disciplinary measure."[38]

When, in 2015, Eastern State Penitentiary in Philadelphia (now a museum) hosted a prison food tasting (throughout the years), they featured nutraloaf for visitors to sample. And not just one, but five different types from across various states and "recipes." After tasting, visitors were encouraged to write down their thoughts on a scorecard and decide whether the practice of serving nutraloaf constitutes a form of cruel and unusual punishment. In videos that appeared on the popular Web site Buzzfeed, you can watch the taste testing in which participants cringe, wince, and even spit out the loaf.[39]

In December 2015, among other prison reforms introduced under the gubernatorial administration of Andrew Cuomo, New York took nutraloaf off the menu. According to the *New York Times*, "experts say no change may have a more immediate impact on prisoners' moods, and on those of the officers assigned to keep them behind bars, than the end of the so-called disciplinary-sanctioned restricted diet."[40]

---

**RECIPE FOR NUTRALOAF[41]**
**SPECIAL MANAGEMENT MEAL**

6 slices whole wheat bread, finely chopped
4 ounces imitation cheese, finely grated
4 ounces raw carrots, finely grated
12 ounces spinach, canned, drained
4 ounces seedless raisins
2 cups Great Northern Beans, cooked and drained
4 tablespoons vegetable oil
6 ounces tomato paste
8 ounces milk, powdered nonfat/skim, instant dried
6 ounces potato flakes dehydrated

Mix all the ingredients together in a 12-quart mixing bowl. Make sure all wet items are drained. Mix until stiff, just moist enough to spread. Form three loaves in glazed bread pans. Place loaf pans in the oven on a sheet pan filled with water, to keep the bottom of the loaves from burning. Bake at 325 degrees in a convection oven for approximately 45 minutes. The loaf will start to pull away from the sides of the bread pan when done.

---

## THE CHOW HALL AND PRISON RIOTS OVER FOOD

Where food is eaten is almost as crucial as what ingredients and components make it up. The prison or jail cafeteria, known colloquially as "the mess hall" or, more commonly, "the chow hall" is simultaneously a site of community and a site of tension: It is one of the daily opportunities for inmates to commune and build bonds, but it is also one of the most tense, highly energized places in the facility. The chow hall is rife with politics, noise, and frustration. It is loud with banging trays, plates, cups, and voices booming. Inmates trying to assert themselves and their place in the institution tend to dominate. Correctional officers watch constantly, and if you are in one of the highest level security prisons, they often stand on the sidelines with guns pointed toward you to ensure that no one gets crazy.

As my inmate friend elaborated:

> The dining hall is a very uncomfortable place. . . . First off, it is segregated into a black section, a white section, a section for child molesters and a section for Latinos . . . the division between sections are obvious and it is a source of tension. Also, they give you very little time to eat, so it is difficult to relax. There is also stress as a result of the fact that there are at least ten guards look[ing] at you while you eat to make sure you're not misbehaving. And, as you leave, there are guards at the door waiting to shake you down to make sure you aren't taking any food with you.[42]

Eating in prison happens early. Breakfast starts around 6 or 6:30 a.m. generally, followed by the midday meal starting around 11 a.m. Dinner is served after an evening count beginning at about 5 p.m. No sharp utensils or objects are allowed to be used by inmates, so that means no sharp knives. Much of the logistics will be reminiscent of high school: You line up outside your cell at meal time and shuffle down, single file to the chow hall, at which point you get in line to receive a tray and are served food buffet-style on a line. New inmates will find that they have trouble figuring out where and who to sit with as the chow hall is one of the most clearly segregated places in the facility: inmates sit based on race or gang affiliation, and new inmates will often get hassled, get their food taken away or find they are not welcome to sit with anyone at first.[43] Getting used to your place in the chow hall is probably secondary to getting your stomach used to the food—many accounts I read say that there is an adjustment period when you start eating prison food, and that your stomach hurts at first, but that eventually you pretty much get used to it.

Speaking of sitting, all the furniture in the chow hall (and, well, basically all of a correctional facility) is bolted to the ground and chained together, so that it cannot be moved or picked up and used as a weapon. Naturally, this furniture favors durability over comfort, so generally inmates are sitting on stool-like seats with hard plastic.

"In general, inmates *hate* eating in the 'chow hall' and much prefer to eat commissary goods in the units," my incarcerated friend told me. In many prisons, the chow hall has even been eliminated due to the fact that it is often a locus of tension between inmates themselves and inmates and guards. A change in timing, quantity, or quality of meals, even on the most minimal scale, can cause major unrest: "Food plays a significant role in prison security. Experienced prison guards know that inmates who are not adequately fed can and do strike out at their captors. Fights can break out from the slightest change in cafeteria procedures."[44] Food is decidedly one of the most often critiqued aspects of the prison experience by inmates. And, in fact, researchers have found a connection between poor food quality and discipline problems and violence.[45]

> As the chow hall door opened, we walked in a single file line, following the four black inmates the Chicanos call mayates. The chow hall was one cavernous rectangular structure with about sixteen stainless steel tables which seat four people. On both sides of the chow hall there was a guard inside a glass cubicle pointing a rifle at us. Behind a cafeteria style glass barrier, a row of four convict kitchen workers moved each tray along, asking if we wanted a certain item on the menu that day.[46]

> One thing I kind of like about the chow hall is I get to hang out with the fellers. Bullshitting with them over a tray of watery biscuit and gravy and soupy oatmeal is a good way to start the day. You see other races make a big show of greeting their kind. Once in a while also, you get to see a fight in the chow hall like the time two sixty-five-year-olds bitch slapped each other. It all started when one of them wanted the other feller's breakfast ham. Instead of asking for it, he stabbed it. The guards in the chow hall couldn't stop laughing. So chow might not be good, but there's always some good bullshit and some good laughs.[47]

## Riots

A prison in Northpoint, Kentucky was completely in flames in 2009. "It's over the food; the food was slop," said one of the guards.[48] Injuring sixteen people and resulting in the destruction of several building units, the riot is purported to have occurred because the food in the prison was intolerably bad and inmates were concerned with the safety and sanitation of the prison kitchen. The food at the time of the riot was under contract, at a price of $2.63 per prisoner, with the private foodservice provider Aramark. "The safety and security risk at that institution was really bad. . . . I've seen whatever they call meatballs, was so hard they couldn't even cut 'em with their sporks."[49] While the prison administrators defended Aramark and the foodservice provided by the prison to its inmates, an investigative report revealed that "almost every prison employee and prisoner who was interviewed cited complaints about food quality and canteen prices as contributing factors to the disturbance."[50]

A group of prisoners in Indonesia in 2006 escaped their confinement by spraying guards in the face and blinding them with a liquid that was steeped in fiery chili peppers.[51] No less than eighteen prisoners made their escape that day, an unprecedented event for the facility. In 2016, the *New York Daily News* reported that melted down Jolly Ranchers are sometimes festooned into dangerous, pointy weapons and plastic spoons are chewed on to create a pointed edge intended to draw blood.[52]

# 6

# The Commissary

The imprisoned self, from inside the walls of the institution, has few ways to regain identity, being under the constant gaze of authority—an authority that expects and waits for rebellion. Carving out sites of resistance is an important part of sustaining selfhood in prison. With the possibilities of subversion deliberately stymied, food becomes one of the few sites ripe for expression and often manifests itself as an attempt to simply reconnect with the world of free will and choice via small pleasures.

Because meals in the chow hall are set and rigid, the only means of this type of escape from the typical prison diet is the window of the commissary—a small store within the prison that sells sundries and foodstuffs, often for quite an expensive cost to prisoners. It is reminiscent of those shops at hotels, tucked in the corner of the lobby, where small hygiene items and snacks sell at an exorbitant amount over what they go for just a few blocks away. As a recent book on prison ramen recipes born of the commissary puts it, "In prison, having money in your commissary account is the difference between the misery that comes with a flavorless, horribly predictable life, where there is little creativity, and one in which you could travel to places of your youth by imitating the meals your mother made."[1]

## HOW THE COMMISSARY WORKS

There are only two above-board ways to eat in prison: either through the dining hall or the commissary. The third way to eat is by smuggling food out of the chow hall and into your bunk or trading smuggled food with other inmates. The commissary is effectively a small prison store, and in fact inmates often call their visits to the commissary "going to the store." Commissary is a privilege that must be earned and maintained, just like any other prison "luxury." Commissary day sounds hectic ("Violence is compulsory on commissary day, it's like those bank panics back in the twenties; people killing each other to be first in line to withdraw money"[2]), and many describe having to wait in lengthy lines to purchase their travel-sized goods. As one inmate put it:

> [On commissary day] order happens sometimes. If outsiders come to inspect our little hellhole or there's a special visitor, suddenly everything is run by the book. On those rare days, commissary runs as smooth as ice. The lady working the store window doesn't close up every twenty minutes for a cigarette break, the cell block sergeant keeps the line full and come the end of the day, everyone has the opportunity to exercise their "privilege," even if they were the very last person in line.[3]

Moreover, the commissary option is only available to inmates with some sort of income, either earned (making, for example, fifteen cents an hour teaching classes or making nameplates) or sent from friends and family via money wire such as Western Union. "People will work all day long doing other people's laundry or cleaning other people's cells. People plead with their 'baby mamas' on the phone to send money so they can eat [from the commissary]."[4]

Prisoners are not allowed to possess cash money inside prison, so even though they may earn some money working, their meager wages are deposited into an account managed by the prison or a prison contractor. Generally, this money, along with whatever a prisoner's family or friends provides to them, is used to purchase goods at the commissary. Typically, prisons allow commissary purchases only once a week and there is a very clear cap on the monthly allowance that an inmate can spend on commissary items. The allowance varies wildly from institution to institution, but very generally seems to max out around $200 to $300 per month, though some sources report figures of $200 per week.

It is also crucial to point out that commissary shopping is not an option for all inmates, due simply to the exorbitant markup on each item. Where everything in the commissary is generally some sort of snack or junk food item, which, on the outside, has very little monetary value, the prison system has made these prices often two- to tenfold the price they would be in any other convenience store. As one inmate wrote about the cost of the commissary as part of the Prison Writing Project, "If your family can take out a second mortgage, you too can be kept stocked in instant coffee and top ramen.[5]

By the same token, having money to use at the commissary is viewed as a sign that a prisoner is cared about and being thought of by those on the outside.[6] With prison labor paying so little, somewhere around ten to seventy-five cents an hour (which many consider inhumane and cruel), coupled with the exorbitant markups at the commissary, it is absolutely necessary to have help from either a friend or family member on the outside giving you money. It is, in fact, the only way to purchase anything substantial. So, when inmates see other inmates with commissary goods, they know that they have a support system on the outside, and this means something: "The shopping bags filled with commissary were a demonstration of family concern, proof that the inmate was being cared for and had not been forgotten."[7]

While much of the money spent in commissaries goes to food, it is also the case that supplemental hygiene items are available, such as deodorant and toothpaste which are not standard issue in every facility. Prisoners have a "tab" or "trust," with which they can buy goods beyond anything provided to them by the institution itself. While the selection is not extensive by any means, inmates buy food at the commissary for many reasons, including meeting dietary needs not provided from dining hall food and also to express freedom through the pleasure of choosing and eating something that is special or different. Prisoners also use the commissary food and creations made from it as sites of community-making or to celebrate occasions. The commissary offers an opportunity for rebellion through choice. And the contents of the commissary create a micro-economy within the prison walls, where its goods turn into currency.

At PEN.org, a platform for writers that are generally oppressed or underrepresented, inmates often talk about their incarceration experiences in a way that is truly eye-opening. One such account was entitled "Commissary Day" by John Adams, who describes the hustle, bustle, and generally necessary evil that is the commissary:

> It's true that the state generally provides for your needs, they feed three meals a day and if you're extremely hungry, you may even find them enjoyable. There are free clothes, water and electricity. . . . Well, sometimes. And what prison doesn't offer shelter? Yes, prison is a little slice of Utopia but to be human is to be infinitely unsatisfied. Now, no one is saying that prisoners are legitimate human beings, but we are similar. Like real people we're slaves to the cravings of our five senses and we still seek what comforts we can find. Only, our longings are probably a bit more intense. We live in an environment designed to deprive the senses. Our world is almost completely devoid of colors, pleasant scents, or tender physical contact. Our senses are starving to death. In such a bland artificial existence, even a simple sugar treat can be mistaken for an exotic ecstasy.
>
> You can't ignore commissary in prison any more than someone in today's society can ignore money. Commissary is money, it is the inmate's currency and purchasing power, it's one of the few means to get those extras that make life a little more bearable. Even guys with no family, no one to give them support of any kind, even they depend on the commissary they cannot buy. Everyone wants some tasty food or at least a tube of toothpaste. Fans, hot pots to warm your water, radios. You can survive without them but I've yet to meet a person who'd want to. Inmates see commissary as a necessity and some of them will go to any lengths to get it. The penitentiary has a separate economy and the commissary is its national bank.[8]

# FCI COMMISSARY LIST

| Name | Reg. No. | Unit | DATE |
|------|----------|------|------|

Only checked items and write-in's will be received – No ADD-ONs OR SUBSTITUTIONS – ALL SALES ARE FINAL

### Register Items

| Item | Price |
|------|-------|
| Copy Card | 5.85 |
| Picture Tickets (limit 10) | 1.00 |

#### Stamps
(Limit $9.40 Total Value)

| Item | Price |
|------|-------|
| Book of Forever Stamps | 9.40 |
| Book of 10 - .01 | 0.10 |
| Book of 10 - .10 | 1.00 |
| Book of 5 - 1.00 | 5.00 |

Specials (Limit 1 - Write in flavor)

|  | |
|------|--|
| Ice Cream _____ | |

### Drinks

| Item | Price |
|------|-------|
| Bottled Water .5L 6pk (2)(K) | 3.75 |
| French Vanilla Cappuccino (2)(K) | 1.40 |
| V-8 Juice (5) | 1.15 |
| Gatorade (5) | 0.90 |
| Cranberry Juice(5) | 1.20 |
| Drink Mix - Sugar Free 8pk (5) | |

(Limit 1 of Each)

| Item | Price |
|------|-------|
| Taster's Choice (K) | 7.80 |
| Coffee Regular (K) | 2.70 |
| Coffee Decaf (K) | 3.30 |
| Rotating Coffee | |
| Decaffeinated Tea (K) | 3.35 |
| Caffeinated Tea | 1.80 |
| Hot Chocolate Regular (K) | 3.75 |
| Hot Chocolate - Sugar Free (SF)(K) | 1.80 |
| Nestea Iced Tea (K) | 2.00 |
| Non-Fat Milk Instant (K) | 3.00 |
| Cherry Drink Mix (K) | 2.15 |
| Drink Mix (K) - Rotating | |

(Limit 3 Total)

| Item | Price |
|------|-------|
| RC Cola (2)* | 2.35 |
| 7-Up (2)* | 2.25 |
| Diet 7-Up (2)* | 2.35 |
| Rotating Soda (2)* | |

(Only 2 of one kind)

### Candy
(Limit 3 of each)

| Item | Price |
|------|-------|
| Hershey's Chocolate Bar (K) | 1.70 |
| Hershey's Almond Bar (K) | 1.70 |
| Caramels | 1.00 |
| Jolly Ranchers - Assorted | 0.85 |
| Jolly Ranchers - Fire | 2.10 |
| Starlite Mints | 0.85 |
| Licorice (K) | 1.30 |
| Sugar Free Candy | |
| Rotating Candy Bars (5) | |
| Rotating Candy | |

#### Soup
(Limit 10 Total)

| Item | Price |
|------|-------|
| Salsa Picante Shrimp (Cup) | 0.55 |
| Thai Noodle Soup (Chili) | 0.70 |
| Ramen | 0.25 |
| _____Beef _____Chicken_____Rotating | |

### Condiments
(Limit 2 of each)

| Item | Price |
|------|-------|
| Non Dairy Creamer (K) | 1.80 |
| Sugar Substitute (K) | 3.75 |
| Rotating Creamer | |

(Limit 1 of each)

| Item | Price |
|------|-------|
| Garlic Powder | 1.30 |
| Onion Powder | 1.30 |
| Seasoned Salt | 1.95 |
| Honey | 2.80 |
| Jalapeno Peppers (K) | 1.90 |
| El Pato Picante | 1.15 |
| Sweet Asian | 1.80 |
| Chili Garlic | 1.50 |
| Salt & Pepper (K) | 1.70 |
| Furikake | 3.75 |
| Mayonnaise (K) | 3.30 |
| Pickles - Kosher (K) | 0.95 |
| Soy Sauce (K) | 1.75 |
| Olive Oil (K) | 2.70 |
| Cream Cheese (10)(K) | 0.35 |
| Jelly | 2.60 |
| Lemon Juice (2) | 1.00 |
| Hershey Syrup | 3.25 |
| Rotating Dip | |
| Rotating Hot Sauce | |

### Food
(Limit 5 each)

| Item | Price |
|------|-------|
| Tuna (K) | 2.75 |
| Salmon | 2.95 |
| Chicken | 3.60 |
| Mackerel | 1.25 |
| Summer Sausage | 1.55 |
| Shredded Beef | 5.85 |
| Spam | 1.25 |
| Beef Bites | 2.30 |
| Turkey Bites | 2.30 |
| White Rice | 0.95 |
| Brown Rice | 1.20 |
| Nacho Cheese Rice (K) | 1.45 |
| Whole Kernel Corn | 1.40 |
| Pepperoni Slices | 2.30 |
| Pizza Kit | 3.65 |
| Taco Mix | 1.95 |
| Tortillas Corn (5 Total) | 1.00 |
| Tortillas Flour (5 Total) | 1.30 |
| Tostadas Corn (2) | 2.40 |
| Refried Beans (3) | 1.30 |
| Chili Beans (3) | 1.45 |
| Beans and Chorizo (3)(K) | 2.05 |
| Oatmeal - Cream Variety (1) | 3.15 |
| Oatmeal - Plain (1) | 1.90 |
| Squeeze Cheese (2) | |
| _____Sharp _____Spicy | |
| Cheese Stick | |
| Creamy Peanut Butter (1)(K) | 2.55 |
| Granola Cereal (1) | |
| Cereal (1) | |
| Rotating Meat | |
| Rotating Spread | |
| Rotating Block Cheese | |

### Snacks
(Limit 3 Total)

| Item | Price |
|------|-------|
| Nacho Cheese Chips | 1.50 |
| Plain Tortilla Chips | 1.90 |
| Pretzels | 1.80 |
| Rotating Potato Chips | |
| Rotating Chip | |

(Limit 1 Each)

| Item | Price |
|------|-------|
| Vanilla Wafers | 2.10 |
| Snack Crackers | 2.05 |
| Cinnamon Honey Grahams (1) | |
| Rotating Crackers (K) | |

(Limit 2 Each)

| Item | Price |
|------|-------|
| Rice Cakes (2) | 3.85 |
| Oreo Cookies (2) | 2.10 |
| Rotating Cookies | |
| Raw Almonds (K) | 3.00 |
| Deluxe Mixed Nuts | 3.15 |
| Trail Mix(3) | 3.10 |
| Cashews - Salted | 1.80 |
| Prunes | 2.70 |
| Marshmallows | 1.95 |
| Pudding 4pk (K) | 2.00 |
| Olives (5)(K) | 1.35 |
| Pork Rinds (5) | 0.95 |
| Popcorn (5)_____Light _____Butter | 0.55 |
| Dried Fruit (3) | 3.00 |
| Party Mix | |
| Pop Tarts (4) | |
| Rotating Pastry | |
| Granola Bars | |
| Protein Bars (5) | 1.75 |
| Breakfast Bar, Rotating(10) | |

### Health Products
(Limit 2 of Each)

| Item | Price |
|------|-------|
| Gas-Ex Cherry | 5.60 |
| Aspirin - Generic 100 | 1.60 |
| Triple Antibiotic Ointment | 4.40 |
| Band-Aids | 0.65 |
| Ben-Gay Ointment | 5.20 |
| Carmex Lip Treatment | 1.70 |
| Chapstick | 3.70 |
| Prilosec Omeprazole | 10.50 |
| Allergy Relief | 1.60 |
| Generic Claritin, Larstadine | 2.60 |
| Acne Treatment | 1.60 |
| Cough Drops | 0.80 |
| Eye Drop | 2.05 |
| Hydrocortisone Cream | 1.25 |
| Hemorrhoid Ointment | 3.85 |
| Ibuprofen | 2.50 |
| Medicated Chest Rub | 2.40 |
| Metamucil Powder | 6.50 |
| Milk of Magnesia | 2.15 |
| Maximum Strength Antacid | 3.40 |
| Pepto Bismol - Generic | 2.60 |
| Generic Zantec, Ranitidine | 5.15 |
| Saline Nasal Spray | 1.85 |
| Tums 3pak | 2.20 |
| Tylenol - Generic | 2.35 |
| Multivitamin | 1.90 |
| Calcium | 2.05 |
| Vitamin B-150 | 3.25 |
| Vitamin C | 1.95 |
| Vitamin E Gelcaps | 2.55 |
| Naproxen Pain Relief | 5.50 |
| Cough Decongestant | 2.20 |

### Dental Products
(Limit 1 of each)

| Item | Price |
|------|-------|
| Close-Up Toothpaste | 1.50 |
| Colgate Toothpaste | 2.45 |
| Sensodyne Toothpaste | 6.75 |
| Dental Floss | 1.25 |
| Denture Baths | 1.95 |
| Denture Toothpaste | 4.05 |
| Denture Brush | 4.40 |
| Fixodent Adhesive | 1.30 |
| Mouthwash | 1.95 |
| Toothbrush Medium | 1.00 |
| Toothbrush Soft | 0.95 |
| Toothbrush Holder | 0.50 |

### Cosmetics
(limit 1 of each)

| Item | Price |
|------|-------|
| Blush Brush | 4.10 |
| Cosmetic Bag | 5.50 |
| Eyebrow Pencil Black | 2.65 |
| Eyebrow Pencil Brown | 2.65 |
| Eye Liner–Liquid Black | 6.05 |
| Eye Liner–Liquid Brown | 6.05 |
| Mascara –Black | 6.90 |
| Mascara Waterproof | 7.30 |
| Lipstick - Color_____ | 5.60 |
| Bronzer - Color_____ | 4.50 |
| Blush | 4.50 |
| Eye Shadow _____ | 7.40 |
| Eye Lash Curler | 5.85 |
| Liquid Make Up _____ | 10.60 |
| Sharpner | 6.55 |
| Make Up Remover Pads | |

(limit 2 of each)

| Item | Price |
|------|-------|
| AAA Battery 4 pk | 1.45 |
| AA Battery 4 pk | 1.45 |
| D Battery 2 pk | 1.75 |

Replacement watch band submit cop-out
Replacement watch batteries submit cop-out

*Image Credit*: Federal Bureau of Prisons—
www.bop.gov/locations/institutions/dub/
DUB_CommList.pdf.

## Laundry Items
(Limit 2 of each)

| | |
|---|---|
| Fabric Dryer Sheets | 3.85 |
| Tide Pods | 7.80 |
| Supremo | 1.50 |
| Rotating Laundry Soap | |

## Recreation Items
(Limit 1 of each)

| | |
|---|---|
| Ankle Brace | 10.80 |
| ____Medium ____Large | |
| Crochet Hooks 6pk | 1.95 |
| 14 X 14 Box | 2.35 |
| Headband | 1.75 |
| Wristband | 1.75 |
| Knee Brace | 10.70 |
| ____Medium ____Large | |
| Polyfill Stuffing | 4.05 |
| Pinochle Playing Cards | 1.65 |
| Poker playing Cards | 1.70 |
| Support Belt | cop-out |
| Weight Gloves | cop-out |
| ____S ____M ____L ____XL | |
| Wrist Support | 8.70 |

## Hair Care
(Limit 1 of each)

| | |
|---|---|
| Suave Shampoo | 1.65 |
| Suave Conditioner | 1.65 |
| Infusium Shampoo | 7.80 |
| Infusium Conditioner | 7.80 |
| Proclaim Shampoo | 4.80 |
| Proclaim Conditioner | 4.80 |
| Rotating Shampoo | |
| Rotating Conditioner | |
| Head & Shoulders Shampoo | 6.40 |
| T-Gel Shampoo | 5.20 |
| Sulfur 8 | 3.85 |
| Wonder 8 Oil | 7.05 |
| Rotating Wrap Lotion | |
| Infusium 23 Treatment | 5.30 |
| Relaxer Regular | 7.80 |
| Hair Dye_____ | 9.10 |
| ____Dark Brown____Black____Blonde____Rotating | |
| Styling Gel | 1.65 |
| Hair Spray | 5.05 |
| Gel Curl Activator | 1.30 |
| AP Growth Oil | 2.85 |
| AP Moisturizer Lotion | 2.85 |
| Ampro Pro Style Gel 6oz | 1.45 |
| Hair Scrunchie | 4.80 |
| Barrettes | 1.50 |
| Detangler Comb | 1.25 |
| Comb and Brush Set | 2.40 |
| Hair Pick | 0.80 |
| Vent Brush | 1.60 |
| Conditioning Caps | 1.75 |
| Shower Caps | 1.60 |
| Claw Clip 3 set, Small | 1.85 |
| Claw Clip 3 set, Large | 3.40 |
| Foam Rollers Small | 1.40 |
| Foam Rollers Medium | 1.35 |
| Foam Rollers Large | 1.35 |
| Du-Rag | 1.70 |
| Quantum Perm | 3.00 |
| Perm Curl Papers | 1.45 |
| Coconut Oil Conditioner | 2.50 |
| AP Magic Gro | 6.55 |
| Hair Mayo | |
| Ponytail Holders | |
| Rotating Pomade | |

## Supplies

| | |
|---|---|
| Address Book (1) | 1.85 |
| Blank Note Cards (no envelope) | 1.50 |
| Bic Ink Pen 2 pack - Black (2) | 1.15 |
| 2 Pencils 4 pack | 0.55 |
| Letter Envelopes - (1 Box)50ct | 1.95 |
| Expansion Folder (1) | 1.50 |
| Swintec Printwheel (2) | 19.40 |
| Swintec Ribbon (2) | 7.25 |
| Swintec Liftoff (2) | 9.25 |
| Legal Size Pad (2) | 1.35 |
| Envelopes - 9x12 yellow (10) | 0.20 |
| Book Light (1) | 12.95 |
| Wireless Notebook | 1.85 |
| Reading Glasses (1) | 4.50 |
| ____1.5 ____2.5 | |
| Typing Paper | 1.90 |

## Foot Care

| | |
|---|---|
| Pedi Paddle & Foot Cream | |
| Corn Cushions (1) | 1.80 |
| Foot Insoles (1) | 2.35 |
| Spenco Arch Cushions 3/4 Length | cop-out |
| ____Size | |
| Shoe Laces 54" (1) | 1.15 |
| ____Black ____White | |
| Tolnaftate Foot Cream (2) | 1.60 |
| Foot Powder 1% Tolnaftate (2) | 2.30 |

## Hygiene Products
(Limit 4 Total)

| | |
|---|---|
| Dial Soap | 1.05 |
| Dove Soap | 1.50 |
| Lever 2000 | 0.95 |

(Limit 1 of each)

| | |
|---|---|
| Tweezers | 2.60 |
| Emery Boards | 0.90 |
| Fingernail Clipper | 0.80 |
| Toenail Clipper | 1.10 |
| Bodywash | 4.10 |
| Neutrogena Soap | 3.40 |
| Soap Dish | 0.45 |
| Dial Roll-On Deodorant | 1.45 |
| Rotating Deodorant | |
| Secret Solid Deodorant | 3.05 |
| Baby Oil | 2.30 |
| Baby Powder | 1.55 |
| St. Ives Lotion | 3.15 |
| Suave Lotion | 2.50 |
| Petroleum Jelly | 1.35 |
| Disposable Razors | 2.15 |
| Noxema | 2.20 |
| Collagen Elastin Moisturizer | 5.50 |
| Oil of Olay | 12.45 |
| Apricot Scrub | 3.90 |
| Ambi Complexion Bar | 2.40 |
| Ambi Skin Fade Cream | 6.10 |
| Cocoa Butter Cream | 5.50 |
| Cotton Swabs | 2.65 |
| Sun Block SPF 30 | 2.15 |
| Gillette Mach 3 System | 10.30 |
| Gillette Mach 3 Cartridges | 13.55 |
| Rotating Lotion | |

## Feminine Hygiene
(Limit 2 of Each)

| | |
|---|---|
| Carefree Panty Liner | 2.40 |
| Miconazole 3 | 10.75 |
| Douche - Vinegar/Water | 1.55 |
| Tampax Regular | 4.15 |
| Tampax Super | 4.15 |
| Always with Wings | 3.90 |

## Shoes
(Limit 1 of each)

| | |
|---|---|
| Shower Shoes | 3.50 |
| ____(5-6) ____(7-8) ____(9-10) ____(11-12) | |
| Clog Slippers | cop-out |
| ____(5.5-6) ____(6.5-7) ____(7.5-8) ____(8.5-9) | |
| ____(9.5-10) | |

## Miscellaneous Items

| | |
|---|---|
| Air Freshener (2) | 1.10 |
| Small Microwave Bowl w/lid (1) | 3.60 |
| Large Bowl w/ Lid | 5.70 |
| Clear Thermal Mug 20oz (1) | 2.70 |
| Clear Thermal Mug 32oz (1) | 3.00 |
| Dish Soap (2) | 1.25 |
| Calculator - Solar (1) | 7.40 |
| Clock Alarm (1) | 8.15 |
| Fan (1)* | 13.00 |
| Dictionary, English (1) | 1.60 |
| Dictionary, Spanish/English (1) | 2.15 |
| Hanger (8) | 0.25 |
| Earbuds | 10.35 |
| Utensil Set (2) | 1.30 |
| Poncho w/hood (1) | 4.95 |
| Watch - (1) | 19.95 |
| Lock (2) | 7.65 |
| Headphones (1) | 34.50 |
| Clear Tunes Radio (1) | 26.90 |
| Sony Radio (1) | 44.85 |
| MP3 Player* (1) | 69.95 |
| MP3 Player Return Envelope | 0.85 |
| Photo Album (1) | 2.90 |
| Mirror - Safety (1) | 1.95 |
| Scissors (1) | 6.45 |
| Sunglasses (1) | 5.20 |
| ID Holder(1) | 1.30 |
| Mesh Commissary Tote | 8.95 |
| Shower Bag | 5.20 |

## Yarn $10.50
(Limit 3 Total)

Must Have Yarn Form from Recreation

## Clothing

| | |
|---|---|
| Gloves (1)* | 0.40 |
| Baseball Cap (1) | 3.90 |
| Robe - One size fits all (1) | 35.10 |
| Robe - Jumbo (3X-4X) (1) | 45.50 |
| Panties - White 3pk (2) | 7.75 |
| Size 5__ 6__ 7__ 8__ | |
| 9__ 10__ 11__ 12__ | |
| Socks - ankle - White Singles (6) | 1.15 |
| Socks Tube (2) | 1.65 |
| Stocking Cap (1) | 2.75 |
| Towel (2) | 5.35 |
| Washcloth (1) | 1.45 |

### Sweatshirt
(Limit 1)

| | |
|---|---|
| ___Sml ___Med ___Lrg ___XL | 15.35 |
| ___2X ___3X ___4X | |
| ___5X | 20.15 |

### Sweatpants
(Limit 1)

| | |
|---|---|
| ___Sml ___Med ___Lrg ___XL | 17.95 |
| ___2X ___3X ___4X | |
| ___5X | 23.40 |

### Gray T-Shirts
(Limit 1)
Select One:

| | |
|---|---|
| Long Sleeve | 10.40 |
| Short Sleeve | 5.75 |
| ___Sml ___Med ___Lrg ___XL | |
| ___2X ___3X ___4X | 7.45 |
| 5X Short Sleeve | 7.55 |
| 5X Long Sleeve | 13.00 |

### Shorts
(Limit 1)

| | |
|---|---|
| ___Small ___Med ___Lrg ___XL | 10.40 |
| ___2X ___3X | 11.70 |
| ___4X ___5X | 15.60 |

### Thermal Shirts
(Limit 1)

| | |
|---|---|
| ___Sml ___Med ___Lrg ___XL | 9.10 |
| ___2X ___3X ___4X ___5X | 10.40 |

### Thermal Pants
(Limit 1)

| | |
|---|---|
| ___Sml ___Med ___Lrg ___XL | 9.10 |
| ___2X ___3X ___4X ___5X | 10.40 |

New Items
_____
_____
_____
_____

***PRICES ARE SUBJECT TO CHANGE***
ALL SALES ARE FINAL
(*) = Items are not transferable between institutions
(K) = Kosher

Andre Matevousian, Warden
Version 06/18/14

# FCI Special Housing Unit

### PLEASE PRINT OR WRITE LEGIBLY OR <u>NO SALE</u>

| Name | Reg. No. | DATE |
|------|----------|------|
|      |          |      |

Only checked items and Readable write-in's will be received - No ADD-ONs – ALL SALES ARE FINAL, Prices Subject to Change Without Notice!

| Stamps | | Hygiene Products | | Health/Medical | |
|--------|--|------------------|--|----------------|--|
| **Stamps** | | **Hygiene Products** | | **Health/Medical** | |
| Book of Forever Stamps (1) | $ 9.40 | Baby Powder | $1.55 | Gas-Ex Cherry | $ 5.60 |
| | | Speed Stick Deodorant (1) | $2.25 | Aspirin - Generic 100 | $ 1.60 |
| | | Anti-Persp (White) | $2.60 | Triple Antibiotic Ointment | $ 4.40 |
| **Drinks** | | Noxema | $2.20 | Band-Aids | $ 0.65 |
| | | Neutrogena Soap | $3.40 | Ben-Gay Ointment | $ 5.20 |
| Coffee Regular (K) | $ 2.70 | Lever 2000 | $0.95 | Carmex Lip Treatment | $ 1.70 |
| Coffee Decaf (K) | $ 3.30 | Dial Soap | $1.05 | Chapstick | $ 2.00 |
| Taster's Choice (K) | $ 7.80 | Soap Dish | $0.45 | Prilosec Omeprazole | $10.50 |
| | | | | Allergy Relief | $ 1.60 |
| **YOU MAY SELECT ONE TYPE OF COFFEE** | | **Hair Care** | | Generic Claritin, Laratadine | $ 2.60 |
| | | (Limit 1 of each) | | Acne Treatment | $ 1.60 |
| **Condiments** | | | | Cough Drops | $ 0.80 |
| | | Suave Shampoo | $1.65 | Eye Drop | $ 2.05 |
| Non Dairy Creamer (K) | $ 1.80 | Suave Conditioner | $1.65 | Hydrocortisone Cream | $ 1.25 |
| Sugar Substitute | $ 3.75 | Head & Shoulders Shampoo | $6.40 | Hemorrhoid Ointment | $ 3.85 |
| | | AP Magic Gro | $6.55 | Ibuprofen | $ 2.50 |
| | | Palm Comb | $0.85 | Medicated Chest Rub | $ 2.40 |
| | | | | Metamucil Powder | $ 6.50 |
| **Food** | | **Miscellaneous Items/Batteries** | | Milk of Magnesia | $ 2.15 |
| (You may select 5 items from list below) | | (Limit 1 of each) | | Maximum Strength Antacid | $ 3.40 |
| | | | | Pepto Bismol - Generic | $ 2.60 |
| Hershey's Chocolate Bar (K) | $ 1.70 | AAA Battery 4PK | $1.45 | Generic Zantec, Ranitidine | $ 5.15 |
| Snack Crackers | $ 2.05 | Legal Size Pad | $1.35 | Saline Nasal Spray | $ 1.85 |
| Squeeze Cheese Sharp | $ 2.95 | Letter Envelopes - 50ct | $1.95 | Tums 3pak | $ 2.20 |
| Granola Cereal | | | | Tylenol - Generic | $ 2.35 |
| Vanilla Wafers | $ 2.10 | **Dental Products** | | Multivitamin | $ 1.90 |
| Rotating Potato Chips | | (Limit 1 of each) | | Calcium | $ 2.05 |
| Oatmeal - Cream Variety | $ 3.15 | | | Vitamin B-150 | $ 3.25 |
| Licorice (K) | $ 1.30 | Close-Up Toothpaste | $1.50 | Vitamin C | $ 1.95 |
| Peanut Butter | $ 2.55 | Fixodent Adhesive | $4.40 | Vitamin E Gelcaps | $ 2.55 |
| | | | | Naproxen Pain Relief | $ 5.50 |
| | | | | Cough Decongestant | $ 2.20 |

All over the counter medications are available in tablet form and will be given to health services for dispensing

**NOTE:** *Inmates on disciplinary segregation status are limited to the items marked with asterisk (\*) only.*
Inmates on Administrative Detention status may purchase all items on this form, but **are not** authorized to add additional items.

CELL #_____ A/D_____ D/S_____ APPROVED_____ DISAPPROVED_____
VERIFIED BY:_____ Date._____
        *OTC Reviewed, By H.S.A.*

APPROVED:_____     DATE_____
**Andre Matevousian, Warden**

Revised 6/18/14

# SCP COMMISSARY LIST

| Name | Reg. No. | Date | Unit |
|------|----------|------|------|
|      |          |      |      |

**Only checked items and write-in's will be received - No ADD-ONs OR SUBSTITUTIONS – ALL SALES ARE FINAL**

**PLEASE PRINT OR WRITE LEGIBLY OR NO SALE**

## Register Items

| Item | Price |
|------|-------|
| Copy Card | 5.85 |
| Picture Tickets (limit 10) | 1.00 |

## Stamps
(Limit $9.40 Total Value)

| Item | Price |
|------|-------|
| Book of Forever Stamps | 9.40 |
| Book of 10 - .01 | 0.10 |
| Book of 10 - .10 | 1.00 |
| Book of 5 - 1.00 | 5.00 |

Specials (Limit 1 - Write in flavor)

Ice Cream _____

## Drinks

| Item | Price |
|------|-------|
| Bottled Water .5L 6pk (2)(K) | 3.75 |
| French Vanilla Cappuccino (2)(K) | 1.40 |
| V-8 Juice (5) | 1.15 |
| Gatorade (5) | 0.90 |
| Cranberry Juice(5) | 1.20 |
| Drink Mix - Sugar Free 8pk (5) | |

(Limit 1 of Each)

| Item | Price |
|------|-------|
| Taster's Choice (K) | 7.80 |
| Coffee Regular (K) | 2.70 |
| Coffee Decaf (K) | 3.30 |
| Rotating Coffee | |
| Decaffeinated Tea (K) | 3.35 |
| Caffeinated Tea | 1.80 |
| Hot Chocolate Regular (K) | 3.75 |
| Hot Chocolate - Sugar Free (SF)(K) | 1.80 |
| Nestea Iced Tea (K) | 2.00 |
| Non-Fat Milk Instant (K) | 3.00 |
| Cherry Drink Mix (K) | 2.15 |
| Drink Mix (K) – Rotating | |

(Limit 3 Total)

| Item | Price |
|------|-------|
| RC Cola (2)* | 2.35 |
| 7-Up (2)* | 2.35 |
| Diet 7-Up (2)* | 2.35 |
| Rotating Soda (2)* | |

(Only 2 of one kind)

## Candy
(Limit 3 of each)

| Item | Price |
|------|-------|
| Hershey's Chocolate Bar (K) | 1.70 |
| Hershey's Almond Bar (K) | 1.70 |
| Caramels | 1.00 |
| Jolly Ranchers - Assorted | 0.85 |
| Jolly Ranchers - Fire | 2.10 |
| Starlite Mints | 0.85 |
| Licorice (K) | 1.30 |
| Sugar Free Candy | |
| Rotating Candy Bars (5) | |
| Rotating Candy | |

## Soup
(Limit 10 Total)

| Item | Price |
|------|-------|
| Salsa Picante Shrimp (Cup) | 0.55 |
| Thai Noodle Soup (Chili) | 0.70 |
| Ramen | 0.25 |
| _____Beef _____Chicken_____Rotating | |

## Condiments
(Limit 2 of each)

| Item | Price |
|------|-------|
| Non Dairy Creamer (K) | 1.80 |
| Sugar Substitute (K) | 3.75 |
| Rotating Creamer | |

(Limit 1 of each)

| Item | Price |
|------|-------|
| Garlic Powder | 1.30 |
| Onion Powder | 1.30 |
| Seasoned Salt | 1.95 |
| Honey | 2.80 |
| Jalapeno Peppers (K) | 1.90 |
| El Pato Picante | 1.15 |
| Sweet Asian | 1.80 |
| Chili Garlic | 1.50 |
| Salt & Pepper (K) | 1.70 |
| Furikake | 3.75 |
| Mayonnaise (K) | 3.65 |
| Pickles - Kosher (K) | 0.95 |
| Soy Sauce (K) | 1.75 |
| Olive Oil (K) | 2.70 |
| Cream Cheese (10)(K) | 0.35 |
| Jelly | 2.60 |
| Lemon Juice (2) | 1.00 |
| Hershey Syrup | 3.25 |
| Rotating Dip | |
| Rotating Hot Sauce | |

## Food
(Limit 5 each)

| Item | Price |
|------|-------|
| Tuna (K) | 2.75 |
| Salmon | 2.95 |
| Chicken | 3.60 |
| Mackerel | 1.25 |
| Summer Sausage | 1.55 |
| Shredded Beef | 5.85 |
| Spam | 1.25 |
| Beef Bites | 2.30 |
| Turkey Bites | 2.30 |
| White Rice | 0.95 |
| Brown Rice | 1.20 |
| Nacho Cheese Rice (K) | 1.45 |
| Whole Kernel Corn | 1.40 |
| Pepperoni Slices | 2.30 |
| Pizza Kit | 3.65 |
| Taco Mix | 1.95 |
| Tortillas Corn (5 Total) | 1.00 |
| Tortillas Flour (5 Total) | 1.40 |
| Tostadas Corn (2) | 2.40 |
| Chili Beans (3) | 1.30 |
| Beans (3) | 1.45 |
| Beans and Chorizo (3)(K) | 2.05 |
| Oatmeal - Cream Variety (1) | 3.15 |
| Oatmeal - Plain (1) | 1.90 |
| Squeeze Cheese (2) | |
| _____Sharp _____Spicy | |
| Cheese Stick | |
| Creamy Peanut Butter (1)(K) | 2.55 |
| Granola Cereal (1) | |
| Cereal (1) | |
| Rotating Meat | |
| Rotating Spread | |
| Rotating Block Cheese | |

## Snacks
(Limit 3 Total)

| Item | Price |
|------|-------|
| Nacho Cheese Chips | 1.50 |
| Plain Tortilla Chips | 1.90 |
| Pretzels | 1.80 |
| Rotating Potato Chips | |
| Rotating Chip | |

(Limit 1 Each)

| Item | Price |
|------|-------|
| Vanilla Wafers | 2.10 |
| Snack Crackers | 2.05 |
| Cinnamon Honey Grahams (1) | 2.15 |
| Rotating Crackers (K) | |

(Limit 2 Each)

| Item | Price |
|------|-------|
| Rice Cakes (2) | 3.85 |
| Oreo Cookies (2) | 2.10 |
| Rotating Cookies | |
| Raw Almonds (K) | 3.00 |
| Deluxe Mixed Nuts | 3.15 |
| Trail Mix(3) | 3.10 |
| Cashews - Salted | 1.80 |
| Prunes | 2.70 |
| Marshmallows | 1.95 |
| Pudding 4pk (K) | 2.00 |
| Olives (5)(K) | 1.35 |
| Pork Rinds (5) | 0.95 |
| Popcorn (5)_____Light _____Butter | 0.55 |
| Dried Fruit (3) | 3.00 |
| Party Mix | |
| Pop Tarts (4) | |
| Rotating Pastry | |
| Granola Bars | |
| Protein Bars (5) | 1.75 |
| Breakfast Bar, Rotating(10) | |

## Health Products
(Limit 2 of Each)

| Item | Price |
|------|-------|
| Gas-Ex Cherry | 5.60 |
| Aspirin - Generic 100 | 1.60 |
| Triple Antibiotic Ointment | 4.40 |
| Band-Aids | 0.65 |
| Ben-Gay Ointment | 5.20 |
| Carmex Lip Treatment | 1.70 |
| Chapstick | 3.70 |
| Prilosec Omeprazole | 10.50 |
| Allergy Relief | 1.60 |
| Generic Claritin, Laratadine | 2.60 |
| Acne Treatment | 1.60 |
| Cough Drops | 0.80 |
| Eye Drop | 2.05 |
| Hydrocortisone Cream | 1.25 |
| Hemorrhoid Ointment | 3.85 |
| Ibuprofen | 2.50 |
| Medicated Chest Rub | 2.40 |
| Metamucil Powder | 6.50 |
| Milk of Magnesia | 2.15 |
| Maximum Strength Antacid | 3.40 |
| Pepto Bismol - Generic | 2.60 |
| Generic Zantec, Ranitidine | 5.15 |
| Saline Nasal Spray | 1.85 |
| Tums 3pak | 2.20 |
| Tylenol - Generic | 2.35 |
| Multivitamin | 1.90 |
| Calcium | 2.05 |
| Vitamin B-150 | 3.25 |
| Vitamin C | 1.95 |
| Vitamin E Gelcaps | 2.55 |
| Naproxen Pain Relief | 5.50 |
| Cough Decongestant | 2.20 |

## Dental Products
(Limit 1 of each)

| Item | Price |
|------|-------|
| Close-Up Toothpaste | 1.50 |
| Colgate Toothpaste | 2.45 |
| Sensodyne Toothpaste | 6.75 |
| Dental Floss | 1.25 |
| Denture Baths | 1.95 |
| Denture Toothpaste | 4.05 |
| Denture Brush | 4.40 |
| Fixodent Adhesive | 1.30 |
| Mouthwash | 1.95 |
| Toothbrush Medium | 1.00 |
| Toothbrush Soft | 0.95 |
| Toothbrush Holder | 0.50 |

## Cosmetics
(limit 1 of each)

| Item | Price |
|------|-------|
| Blush Brush | 4.10 |
| Cosmetic Bag | 5.50 |
| Eyebrow Pencil Black | 2.65 |
| Eyebrow Pencil Brown | 2.65 |
| Eye Liner–Liquid Black | 6.05 |
| Eye Liner–Liquid Brown | 6.05 |
| Mascara –Black | 6.90 |
| Mascara Waterproof | 7.30 |
| Lipstick - Color_____ | 5.60 |
| Bronzer - Color_____ | 4.50 |
| Blush | 4.50 |
| Eye Shadow _____ | 7.40 |
| Eye Lash Curler | 5.85 |
| Liquid Make Up _____ | 10.60 |
| Sharpner | 6.55 |
| Make Up Remover Pads | |

## Batteries
(limit 2 of each)

| Item | Price |
|------|-------|
| AAA Battery  4 pk | 1.45 |
| AA Battery  4 pk | 1.45 |
| D Battery  2 pk | 1.75 |

Replacement watch band submit cop-out
Replacement watch batteries submit cop-out

## Laundry Items
(Limit 2 of each)

| | |
|---|---|
| Fabric Dryer Sheets | 3.85 |
| Tide Pods | 7.80 |
| Country Save 5 pack | 2.55 |
| Rotating Laundry Soap | |

## Recreation Items
(Limit 1 of each)

| | |
|---|---|
| Ankle Brace   (Submit Cop-Out) | 10.80 |
| ____Medium ____Large | |
| Crochet Hooks 6pk | 1.95 |
| 14 X 14 Box | 2.35 |
| Headband | 1.75 |
| Wristband | 1.75 |
| Knee Brace   (Submit Cop-Out) | 10.70 |
| ____Medium ____Large | |
| Pinochle Playing Cards | 1.65 |
| Poker playing Cards | 1.70 |
| Support Belt | cop-out |
| Weight Gloves | cop-out |
| ____S ____M ____L ____XL | |
| Wrist Support | 8.70 |

## Hair Care
(Limit 1 of each)

| | |
|---|---|
| Suave Shampoo | 1.65 |
| Suave Conditioner | 1.65 |
| Infusium Shampoo | 7.80 |
| Infusium Conditioner | 7.80 |
| Proclaim Shampoo | 4.80 |
| Proclaim Conditioner | 4.80 |
| Rotating Shampoo | |
| Rotating Conditioner | |
| Head & Shoulders Shampoo | 6.40 |
| T-Gel Shampoo | 5.20 |
| Sulfur 8 | 3.85 |
| Pink Hair Oil | |
| Rotating Wrap Lotion | |
| Infusium 23 Treatment | 5.30 |
| Relaxer Regular | 7.80 |
| Hair Dye____ | 9.10 |
| ____Dark Brown____Black____Blonde____Rotating | |
| Styling Gel | 1.65 |
| Hair Spray | 5.85 |
| Gel Curl Activator | 1.30 |
| AP Growth Oil | 2.85 |
| AP Moisturizer Lotion | 2.85 |
| Ampro Pro Style Gel 6oz | 1.45 |
| Hair Scrunchie | 4.80 |
| Barrettes | 1.50 |
| Detangler Comb | 1.25 |
| Comb and Brush Set | 2.40 |
| Hair Pick | 0.80 |
| Vent Brush | 1.60 |
| Conditioning Caps | 1.75 |
| Shower Caps | 1.60 |
| Claw Clip 3 set, Small | 1.85 |
| Claw Clip 3 set, Large | 3.40 |
| Foam Rollers Small | 1.40 |
| Foam Rollers Medium | 1.35 |
| Foam Rollers Large | 1.35 |
| Du-Rag | 1.70 |
| Quantum Perm | 3.00 |
| Perm Curl Papers | 1.45 |
| Coconut Oil Conditioner | 2.50 |
| AP Magic Gro | 6.55 |
| Hair Mayo | 4.50 |
| Ponytail Holders | |
| BeesWax | 2.10 |

## Supplies

| | |
|---|---|
| Address Book (1) | 1.85 |
| Blank Note Cards (no envelope) | 1.50 |
| Bic Ink Pen 2 pack - Black (2) | 1.15 |
| 2 Pencils 4 pack | 0.55 |
| Letter Envelopes - (1 Box)50ct | 1.95 |
| Expansion Folder (3) | 1.50 |
| Swintec Printwheel (2) | 19.40 |
| Swintec Ribbon (2) | 7.25 |
| Swintec Liftoff (2) | 9.25 |
| Legal Size Pad (2) | 1.35 |
| Envelopes - 9x12 yellow (10) | 0.20 |
| Book Light (1) | 12.95 |
| Wireless Notebook | 1.85 |
| Reading Glasses (1) | 4.50 |
| ____1.5 ____2.5 | |
| Typing Paper | 1.90 |

## Foot Care

| | |
|---|---|
| Pedi Paddle & Foot Cream | |
| Corn Cushions (1) | 1.80 |
| Foot Insoles (1) | 2.35 |
| Spenco Arch Cushions 3/4 Length | cop-out |
| ____Size | |
| Shoe Laces 54" (1) | 1.15 |
| ____Black ____White | |
| Tolnaftate Foot Cream (2) | 1.60 |
| Foot Powder 1% Tolnaftate (2) | 2.30 |

## Hygiene Products
(Limit 4 Total)

| | |
|---|---|
| Dial Soap | 1.05 |
| Rotating Soap | |
| Lever 2000 | 0.95 |
| No Scent Soap | |

(Limit 1 of each)

| | |
|---|---|
| Tweezers | 2.60 |
| Emery Boards | 0.90 |
| Fingernail Clipper | 0.80 |
| Toenail Clipper | 1.10 |
| Bodywash | 4.10 |
| Neutrogena Soap | 3.40 |
| Soap Dish | 0.45 |
| Dial Roll-On Deodorant | 1.45 |
| Ladies Speed Stick | 2.45 |
| Rotating Deodorant | |
| Baby Oil | 2.30 |
| Baby Powder | 1.55 |
| St. Ives Lotion | 3.15 |
| Suave Lotion | 2.50 |
| Rotating Lotion | |
| Petroleum Jelly | 1.35 |
| Disposable Razors | 2.15 |
| Noxema | 2.20 |
| Collagen Elastin Moisturizer | 5.50 |
| Oil of Olay | 12.45 |
| Apricot Scrub | 3.90 |
| Ambi Complexion Bar | 2.40 |
| Ambi Skin Fade Cream | 6.10 |
| Cocoa Butter Cream | 5.50 |
| Cotton Swabs | 2.65 |
| Sun Block | 2.15 |
| Gillette Mach 3 System | 10.30 |
| Gillette Mach 3 Cartridges | 13.55 |

## Feminine Hygiene
(Limit 2 of Each)

| | |
|---|---|
| Carefree Panty Liner | 2.40 |
| Miconazole 3 | 10.75 |
| Douche - Vinegar/Water | 1.55 |
| Tampax Regular | 4.15 |
| Tampax Super | 4.15 |
| Always with Wings | 3.90 |

## Shoes
(Limit 1 of each)

| | |
|---|---|
| Shower Shoes | 3.50 |
| ____(5-6) ____(7-8) ____(9-10) ____(11-12) | |
| Clog Slippers   (Submit Cop-Out) | |
| ____(5.5-6) ____(6.5-7) ____(7.5-8) ____(8.5-9) | |
| ____(9.5-10) | |
| Crocks   (Submit Cop-Out) | |
| ____(Sml) ____(Med) ____(Lrg) | |

## Miscellaneous Items

| | |
|---|---|
| Locker Organizer | 11.65 |
| Air Freshener (2) | 1.10 |
| Small Microwave Bowl w/lid (1) | 3.60 |
| Large Bowl w/ Lid | 5.70 |
| Clear Thermal Mug 20oz (1) | 2.70 |
| Clear Thermal Mug 32oz (1) | 3.00 |
| Dish Soap (2) | 1.70 |
| Calculator - Solar (1) | 7.40 |
| Clock Alarm (1) | 8.15 |
| Fan (1)* | 13.00 |
| Dictionary, English (1) | 1.60 |
| Dictionary, Spanish/English (1) | 2.15 |
| Hanger (8) | 0.25 |
| Earbuds | 10.35 |
| Utensil Set (2) | 1.30 |
| Poncho w/hood (1) | 4.95 |
| Watch - (1) | 19.95 |
| Lock (2) | 7.65 |
| Headphones (1) | 34.50 |
| Clear Tunes Radio (1) | 26.90 |
| Sony Radio (1) | 44.85 |
| MP3 Player* (1) | 69.95 |
| MP3 Player Return Envelope | 0.85 |
| Photo Album (1) | 2.90 |
| Mirror - Safety (1) | 1.95 |
| Scissors (1) | 6.45 |
| Sunglasses (1) | 5.20 |
| ID Holder(1) | 1.30 |
| Mesh Commissary Tote | 8.95 |
| Shower Bag | 5.20 |
| Body Puff | |

**Yarn $10.50**

(Limit 3 Total)

**Polyfill Stuffing $4.05**

(Limit 1 Total)

**Must Have Yarn Form from Recreation**

## Clothing

| | | | |
|---|---|---|---|
| Gloves (1)* | | | 0.40 |
| Baseball Cap (1) | | | 3.90 |
| Robe - One size fits all (1) | | | 35.10 |
| Robe - Jumbo (3X-4X) (1) | | | 45.50 |
| Panties - White 3pk (2) | | | 7.75 |
| Size 5___ 6___ 7___ 8___ | | | |
| 9___ 10___ 11___ 12___ | | | |
| Socks - ankle - White Singles (6) | | | 1.15 |
| Socks Tube (2) | | | 1.65 |
| Scarf (1) | | | 6.65 |
| Stocking Cap (1) | | | 2.75 |
| Towel (2) | | | 5.35 |
| Washcloth (2) | | | 1.45 |

### Sweatshirt

| | | | | |
|---|---|---|---|---|
| ___Sml ___Med ___Lrg ___XL | | | | 15.35 |
| ___2X ___3X ___4X | | | | |
| ___5X | | | | 20.15 |

### Sweatpants
(Limit 1)

| | | | | |
|---|---|---|---|---|
| ___Sml ___Med ___Lrg ___XL | | | | 17.95 |
| ___2X ___3X ___4X | | | | |
| ___5X | | | | 23.40 |

### Pajamas - Top
(Limit 1)

| | | | | |
|---|---|---|---|---|
| ___Sml ___Med ___Lrg ___XL | | | | |
| ___2X ___3X ___4X | | | | |
| ___5X | | | | |

### Pajamas - Bottom
(Limit 1)

| | | | | |
|---|---|---|---|---|
| ___Sml ___Med ___Lrg ___XL | | | | |
| ___2X ___3X ___4X | | | | |
| ___5X | | | | |

(Limit 1)
Select One:

| | | | | |
|---|---|---|---|---|
| Long Sleeve | | | | 10.40 |
| Short Sleeve | | | | 5.75 |
| ___Sml ___Med ___Lrg ___XL | | | | |
| ___2X ___3X ___4X | | | | 7.45 |
| 5X Short Sleeve | | | | 7.55 |
| 5X Long Sleeve | | | | 13.00 |

### Shorts
(Limit 1)

| | | | | |
|---|---|---|---|---|
| ___Small ___Med ___Lrg ___XL | | | | 10.40 |
| ___2X ___3X | | | | 11.70 |
| ___4X ___5X | | | | 15.60 |

### Thermal Shirts
(Limit 1)

| | | | | |
|---|---|---|---|---|
| ___Sml ___Med ___Lrg ___XL | | | | 9.10 |
| ___2X ___3X ___4X ___5X | | | | 10.40 |

### Thermal Pants
(Limit 1)

| | | | | |
|---|---|---|---|---|
| ___Sml ___Med ___Lrg ___XL | | | | 9.10 |
| ___2X ___3X ___4X ___5X | | | | 10.40 |

### New Items

_____

_____

_____

_____

_____

_____

***PRICES ARE SUBJECT TO CHANGE***
ALL SALES ARE FINAL
(*) = Items are not transferable between institutions
(K) = Kosher

VERIFIED BY:_____

OTC REVIEWED, BY H.S.A

_____

**Andre Matevousian, Warden**
Version 06/18/14

## CELEBRITIES AND THE COMMISSARY

Celebrities in prison are a fascination of society, likely because we know that in the real world they generally live in the lap of luxury, having anything and everything they desire on a whim. While doing time for the average person is incredibly difficult, it is even more puzzling to think about how celebrities get by in prison. That is especially true when it comes to food. The following accounts for what was dug up about celebrities feeding themselves in prison. The reason that this section has landed in this chapter about the commissary in particular is because an almost universal theme while researching celebrities dining in prison is that they (a) complain a lot about the food and (b) many of them eat almost exclusively from the commissary.

The rapper Dwayne Michael Carter, Jr., better known as Lil Wayne, was sentenced to a year in prison on Rikers Island just outside of New York City. Prison records, obtained by TMZ, reveal Lil Wayne requested from the commissary list some Tropical Punch Kool Aid, Cool Ranch Doritos, Nacho Cheese Doritos, and chocolate chip cookies.[9] Of course, Lil Wayne had plenty of people sending him money for anything he wanted from the commissary, and, compared to other inmates, he did not spend that long incarcerated. It is reported that during one of her multiple incarcerations, this one in 2010, actress Lindsay Lohan lived on Jell-O pudding alone, because it was the only thing that came "packaged."[10] And craft maven/home décor magnate Martha Stewart reportedly lost around ten pounds by "trying to not eat the bad food" after serving a lengthy sentence in a federal penitentiary in 2004.[11] She later even claimed that there is a need for prison reform, specifically stating that the women she did time with were not given any opportunities for rehabilitation or skill-garnering. Other sources say that she dabbled in microwave cooking during her time incarcerated. This contention should be viewed with skepticism simply because microwave access is quite rare for inmates.

Though not a famous actor, but famous for making many people rich in an elaborate Ponzi scheme, the fraudster that captured the country's attention Bernie Madoff has been in prison since his conviction in 2010. A piece on Madoff's life behind bars appeared in *NY Magazine*, claiming that he had hired an inmate to do his laundry for $8 a month, despite the fact that the going rate was generally $10 ("Bernie was cheap").[12] The article then goes on to describe Madoff's commissary tendencies: "Once a week, Madoff takes his place on the commissary line, turning in his checklist of goodies to buy. . . . Macaroni and cheese, one of Madoff's favorite meals, costs 60 cents, and a can of Madoff's preferred drink, Diet Coke, is a bargain at 45 cents."[13]

*Real Housewives of New Jersey* star Teresa Giudice's prison diaries were published online by *Us Weekly* during her stint in a federal correctional institution in

Danbury, Connecticut (Giudice and her husband were charged on forty-one counts of fraud in 2014). She, like many of her celebrity counterparts, takes issue with the food, but a surprising twist is her claim that she is being overfed—something I did not come across very often in my research. She says, "I went to lunch at 10:20. I had tater tots, a soy burger that was so gross and orange! I also had some potato salad. They feed us so much here. I'm going to have potatoes coming out of my ears pretty soon!"[14] Her commissary list, obtained by TMZ, consisted of: Cilantro cubes, Oreos, Albacore tuna, Dove bars, deli meat, Louisiana hot sauce, hummus, and wild berry frozen yogurt.[15]

Any discussion of celebrities in prison seems incomplete without the rock star anecdote. Luckily, a recently published book called *Prison Ramen* came out, with a forward by Samuel L. Jackson, to capture details around some of the most notorious of prison meals: the spread. The book features a story from Guns N' Roses guitarist Slash, who ended up in jail in the early days of the band. After the band van was pulled over in a routine traffic stop, Slash was detained for an outstanding jaywalking ticket.[16] While not very rock 'n' roll, he picked up a simple ramen recipe at the Louisiana county jail that has apparently stuck with him on the tour bus ever since.[17]

Contemporary actor and director Shia LaBeouf contributed to the *Prison Ramen* book with a recipe for "Egg Ramen Salad Sandwich"—a dish he learned during his ninth incarceration.[18] While nine lock-ups seems tough, LaBeouf's total time behind bars is less than a week or two all told, but he calls this egg sandwich concoction "terrific" and includes a detailed recipe:

## SHIA LABEOUF'S EGG RAMEN SALAD SANDWICH

| | |
|---|---|
| 1 pack chicken flavor Ramen | 2 tablespoons mayonnaise |
| 1 cup boiling water | 1 hoagie or hero roll, split open |
| 3 hard-boiled eggs, chopped | 2 slices American cheese |

1. Crush the Ramen in the wrapper and empty into a bowl. Set aside the seasoning packet.
2. Add the water, cover, and let sit for about 5 minutes.
3. Drain off excess water. Add the seasoning and mix well.
4. Combine the eggs and mayonnaise in a separate bowl. Mash and mix well with a fork.
5. Add the Ramen. Mix well.
6. Open the roll and place the cheese in it.
7. Fill the roll with the Ramen egg salad.

## SITES OF EXPRESSION: SPREAD, BOWLS, NACHOS

While so much of prison food is banal and repetitive, the commissary is often a portal to a bit of expression, albeit quite limited itself. Through the window of the commissary exists a multitude of combinations that can be concocted based on what is sold.

Inmates exercise their individuality and remember connections to the outside world by getting creative with their commissary items. Sure, some inmates simply eat the food as it is, such as Fritos or a Jell-O pudding cup. But much more fascinating is when they utilize the "ingredients" from the commissary to make creative recipes. Sometimes called making "a spread," "spreading," or making "a bowl," these meals involve bringing together the limited ingredients of commissary (or "canteen") items or leftovers smuggled out of the chow hall at a meal earlier in the day and transforming them into innovative concoctions. They force unbelievable feats of creativity: Need garlic? You squeeze it from garlic supplement pills. Need a "pot" to cook your food in? Get someone that works in the kitchen to smuggle a huge empty tuna can out for you. In addition to the incredible ingenuity required to make your own prison meals, these are opportunities for inmates to escape the rigidity of the routine, the typically bland food of the chow hall, and the repetitiveness of the cuisine. As Sandra Cate's captivating article on spreading in a 2007 issue of *Gastronomica* explains about the use of the commissary at the San Francisco county jail, "Spread . . . reflects personal taste and individual access to resources. As such, it is an inmate's product of choice, not under the control of any authority. And, of course, handcrafted, not mass-produced by an institution serving nearly eight hundred men."[19] Her article, which was written based on interviews and photography taken by her husband Robert Gumpert (some of whose images are featured here), explains the importance of these creations not just as a literal taste of the outside, but as a moment of color, flavor, and expression counter to the institution. "The value and significance of spread to inmates can be understood only within the larger contexts of confinement and the institutional diet. Inmate interviews suggested an oppositional, even dialectical, relation between official food and spread, as food served on the official trays during the day is transformed into spread later that evening."[20] The basis of many of the savory recipes created from commissary items involves Top Ramen noodles. Ramen is above all else the basis of spreading.

Online, I found many accounts of inmates discussing the ways in which they were making commissary items into their own snacks and meals. Additionally, a few cookbooks have been published from prisoners seeking to share their world behind bars with the public, including *From the Big House to Your House* and *Prison Ramen*. In prison cells, meals and treats are generally made with only a hotpot, if even that, and these hotpots do not always fully boil water for safety reasons. ID cards are used to chop things, as knives are never allowed. Chip bags are saved and used to boil things in. It's part re-creating what one used to do on the outside and part imagination, attempting to come close to the flavors of home and the outside world.

"Ingenuity" is probably the word that I would use if I had to sum up the ways that I have read about prisoners making food on their own. What it seems to take is a special combination of creativity, knowledge (often passed-on or experience-based), cooking skill, technical skill, and sheer boredom to come up with what these inmates concoct. One inmate told his story in the book *Fourth City*, wanting to recreate some of the recipes he used to make with his grandmother in his youth. When he came up short on flour, he had to be extremely innovative:

> [Getting] flour was another story. This took more creative thinking on my part. So, as I lay there in my hot, stifling cell, I came up with an idea. Using items I had stored in the plastic bin under my bed, I took a box of macaroni and cheese, emptied the noodles into a bowl, and filled it with cold water. I let the pasta soak for around half an hour, checking it every ten minutes, until I got my desired texture (think Play-Doh). Then, I drained the water and grabbed fistfuls of pasta, squeezing them through my fingers by opening and closing my hand until I had a mound of wet, doughy pasta. But the dough was too sticky. I took some Cheez-It crackers and placed them inside an empty potato-chip bag. With an unopened can of beans, I crushed the crackers into dust. I slowly incorporated it into the dough. This made the dough more pliable (and added a hint of cheese flavor to the dough). Now, with the dough complete, the work began.[21]

## SITES OF COMMUNITY-MAKING: SPREADING WITH OTHERS

Commissary items are much more than just snacks to prisoners. As outlined above, they provide an opportunity for creativity, expression, and harken back to the real world with this connection being forged by food. But in another way, the commissary shows us how prison foodways, specifically through use of commissary items, are used to construct social relationships, build community, and break bread together. "While a single inmate may make the spread, the process more often involves complex social arrangements in terms of collective contributions and the final sharing."[22] Making "a spread" or "a bowl," "a nacho," or "a noodle," especially collectively (banding the resources of a few inmates together), reasserts a sense of self and builds community.

Amy B. Smoyer's interviews with thirty formerly incarcerated women shows the vital role that commissary plays in building social networks through food. Her interviews revealed that women in prison spend time passing food knowledge among each other, whether it be cooking techniques, recipes, or how to get "in" with the women that work in the kitchen and have access to a larger variety of foodstuffs ("If you worked in the kitchen, people were nice to you anyway because they knew you had access to a lot of things they would never be able to get").[23] Smuggling was also equated with stature in building hierarchies among female inmates (and this seems to ring true generally to all incarcerated peoples): Those that could smuggle well often gained respect and favor with other inmates, mostly because they were able to cook the most exotic and exciting dishes with their rarer items.[24] Overall, as Smoyer notes, "Among inmates, control of foodways knowledge, skills, and/or resources was a sign of strength that could translate into social power. Participants described cooking groups and cafeteria experiences as foodways through which inmates organized themselves and built relationships."[25]

My friend wrote me from prison:

> The most common thing people make together [from the commissary] are giant nachos. One guy will buy chips and cheese; another might buy a beef log and salsa, etc. To get in on a nacho, you need to contribute $5–10 worth of food, which means that most people only do this on special occasions like birthdays. . . . People really look forward to nacho nights and they will often say with a sense of pride that they are not going to the dining hall.[26]

---

**CLASSIC SPREAD FEAST**

6/8 ramen picante beef soups
1 pk black bean flakes
1 pk refried beans
1 pk beef stew

4 spicy/beef summer sausages
1 cup cheese powder or 4/5 jalapeno
    squeeze cheese

Cook up soups/beans/stew. Dice and heat sausages, mix together with cheese. Portion out and serve.[27]

---

Inmates at San Francisco County Jail prepare "spread" and an "apple pie." *Photo Credit:* Robert Gumpert

## RECIPES

Here are some accounts from various inmates discussing the ways they get creative with commissary fare as well as some recipes from books and across the Internet.

If you are lucky your family or friends send you a little commissary money. You are allowed to spend $75.00 every two weeks. You can buy a radio, typewriter, fan, hot pot, headset, watch. Also hygienes, cause they do not offer you deodorant, shampoo, shower shoes, mouthwash, lotions. Also food, because the food is so bad. You definitely want to buy a case of ramen soups for $6.00, cause you can survive on them babies. A lot of men buy them. I also buy tuna, jalapeno peppers, cookies and vitamins. A lot of guys fix Prison Tacos, mixing different types of food together to place on flour tortillas. You take a pouch of chili, beef pot roast, or beef tips, throw in some chips, ramen soup, peppers and cheese, and you have something really darn good. Beats the tray every day. You place everything in a bag, yell at the guy you offered on eating with that night or day, and he shoots his fishing line down to you. You fish the end in, place the bag on his line, he pulls it back to his cell. We have a little open space at the bottom of the door, big enough to pull some food in, or newspaper. You even got Tuna tacos: Tuna, ramen soup, salad dressing, peppers, pickles, cheese, and chips. There is some really good cooks back here.[28]

I got four or five bowls. Start off with your two Top Ramen noodles in a small bag. Put hot water in them, but don't put too much. Mix them around until you get that nice feel, like it is smooth and the noodles cooked. Mix in a bag of hot chips (Hot Cheese Crunchies), adding more water if the cheese crunch sucks up some of the water. Keep this on the side. I don't like beef jerky, but if you like it you can add it in at that moment. Pour two packages of Jalapeño Cheese Squeezer ("squeeze cheese") into a bowl, mix it with a cool amount of milk, enough so that it will spread, so you can spread it over your nachos. Rip open a package of chili beans and pour it into another bowl. Chop up a regular or hot pickle into small dice pieces. You now have, in separate bowls, noodles, cheese, chili beans, and pickle. Throw the cheese and beans into the microwave and let them warm up to a nice, wonderful temperature, at least five minutes. Make sure you watch them in case they overboil. If they overboil, open the microwave door, mix them up, and warm them up about three more minutes. Take them out, run to whatever table you're at. Lay down a flat bag. Put tortilla chips or Doritos down first. Pour the noodles with the hot chips over that, then the beans, but slowly, making sure there's a rim of nacho chips around the spread. Once I got the beans down, I pour the pickles, 'cause I got them slice and dice. I pour the pickles nice and rice over it, then I pour the cheese on top of that. Once I got the cheese on top of it then it's cool, and that's what I be calling my Nacho Spread.[29]

I made a burrito or Bomb Chino as I call them. You mix one individual serving of crushed corn chips, one crushed noodle soup, one crushed bag of BBQ potato chips together in a plastic bag—[thoroughly] combine these fine gourmet items then add one to 1½ cups of hot water to the bag, mix [thoroughly], evenly and seal the bag wrapping in a towel or a month old newspaper. Let sit for 15 to 30 minutes unless you're starving. Empty the contents into a paper plate, paper bag, or anything somewhat clean. Eat with a fairly clean plastic spoon. It's a delight in convict cuisine. Add spices, meats, vegetables as available to suit your own tastes![30]

## PRISON CHEESECAKE (EXCERPT FROM *ORANGE IS THE NEW BLACK*)

1. Prepare a crust of crushed graham crackers mixed with four pats of margarine stolen from the dining hall. Bake it in a Tupperware bowl for about a minute in the microwave, and allow it to cool and harden.
2. Take one full round of Laughing Cow cheese, smash with a fork, and mix with a cup of vanilla pudding until smooth.
   Gradually mix in one whole container of Cremora, even though it seems gross. Beat viciously until smooth. Add lemon juice from the squeeze bottle until the mixture starts to stiffen. Note: this will use most of the plastic lemon.
3. Pour into the bowl atop the crust, and put on ice in your bunkie's cleaning bucket to chill until ready to eat.

It was a little squishy the first time; I should have used more lemon juice. But it was a great success. Yvette raised her eyebrows when she tasted it. "Buena!" she proclaimed. I was very proud.

## PIZZA BURGER[31]

### Ingredients
- Microwavable single serve frozen pizza
- Microwavable double cheeseburger

### Directions
Cook pizza in microwave as directed. Cook cheeseburger in microwave as directed. Put pizza between meat of cheeseburger.

Best eaten with: bag of chips, candy bar, and soft drink.

## BEVERAGES

Prison wine, also known as "pruno," is infamous; the lore includes rumors that it is made in the toilet, which, on desperate occasions, seems to be true, though it is unlikely that the practice is frequent, given that prisoners need to relieve themselves on a daily basis and the fermentation process for alcohol is long.

Patience is another key factor in commissary creations: trial and error are necessary and some recipes call for weeks of waiting. Pruno is such an item. From my understanding, pruno is harder to make these days because of the rarity of fresh fruits, which it requires. But if you do manage to fake being Jewish, get a kosher meal, receive a fresh piece of fruit, and smuggle it out of the cafeteria, you are on your way to making pruno.

According to other sources, "Pruno can also be boiled and distilled in a hot pot to make a cheap form of whiskey affectionately called 'White Lightning.' Highly potent and bitingly sour, White Lightning can go for $25 a cup, depending on the quality."[33]

---

**PRUNO RECIPE[32]**

10 peeled oranges cut into wedges
10 browned, soft apples cut into wedges
1 cup Sugar in the Raw
1 yeast packet
16 oz and 1 cup warm water
8 oz can of fruit cocktail
1 packet of raisins

1. Combine the fruit cocktail, apples, raisins and oranges in a 1-gallon Ziploc bag and mash them up taking care to not pop the bag. Once the fruit is beaten into a pulp, add the raw sugar and mix.
2. Add the 16 ounces of warm water to the bag and then seal it. Submerge the sealed bag in a sink of warm water for 15 minutes.
3. In a bowl mix the yeast packet with a cup of warm water and 3 teaspoons of raw sugar and wait til it froths up. Add this to the bag of mushy fruit then store in a dark place.
4. Every day for seven to eight days pour warm water (not hot) over the bag then wrap it in a towel and store. Never allow the bag to cool, else the yeast will die.
5. As part of the fermenting process, the bag will bloat up from the carbon dioxide so you'll need to burp it by opening the bag and releasing the carbon dioxide. Repeat this process every day until there's no longer any bloating.
6. Filter the contents through a cheesecloth.

# 7

❖ ❖

# Prison Gardens, Culinary Training, and Examples from Abroad

This book would be remiss to consider the future of food in prison and not attempt to envision what potential solutions exist to change the system. What is most striking about the current paradigm is that it fails to take into account the impactful way in which food can touch and change the lives of the incarcerated. The current system of corrections seems, as mentioned many times throughout this book, to simply satiate prisoners at the most basic level, for the cheapest price, and with the most convenience. While this is understandable based on the sheer volume of food served per day, it is still an unfortunate missed opportunity. For example, if a person is given a thirteen-year sentence, that means they are eating approximately 14,235 meals in prison over their time incarcerated. One could argue that this is 14,235 currently missed opportunities.

Food in prison is at its best underwhelming, and cruel at its worst. It keeps prisoners in a place of overall malaise and dissatisfaction with regard to their mealtimes, so they turn to the commissary where they are up-charged for a small bit of taste pleasure—not a great return on investment ratio. Additionally, the current state of prison food often creates tension, breeds corruption, solidifies hierarchy, and itself *generates* a host of overall problems for these institutions. Through the creation of micro-economies, food becomes currency, which would not be so highly valued (and therefore not so highly divisive) if the status quo meal were more satisfying. As with school food, or even the current food system in general, our country can likely do better with prison food and even be impactful. In so doing, we could begin to understand the vital role that food currently plays in the correctional system. As Bryan Finoki said in *GOOD Magazine* online:

> if people are what they eat, and (more so) are what they are made to eat, then the inmate is quite literally the product of the prison system itself. Food is nothing more than grease for the cogs of a systemic mechanical redesign of the inmate, controlled at the most fundamental level. . . . Despite the Federal Bureau of Prison's national menu and the justice system's previous rulings against the Nutraloaf as any kind of cruel and unusual punishment, food seems to be a critical and neglected lens for looking into current interpretations of the state's obligation to its incarcerated population.[1]

As with every broken system, there are those within it trying to make it right and turn the corner; the prison food issue is no exception. Not only are excellent strides being made to create prison gardens and culinary programs in the United States, but examples from abroad tell us that a greater breadth of trust about food and prison life in general can yield a fruitful result, such as less internal violence and lower recidivism rates. This chapter discusses those prison gardens and farms as well as examples of prisons from abroad that are treating food differently than we do in the American system.

## PRISON GARDENS AND FARMS

Prison gardening and farming programs teach inmates about food, nutrition, self-care, and community-building therefore lending hands-on, experiential benefits that remain skills for life. It should come as no surprise that humans who lack meaningful connection to other people and a healthy environment are more likely to act outside of agreed-upon social conventions. As discussed, people who end up in prison are then subjected to a draconian model of punishment that is based on further isolation and removal from the natural elements of life. Modern society itself has largely distanced itself from the natural world, replacing interaction with the wildness of the elements, animals, and nature with increasingly artificial environments.[2] As more and more of the elements that connect us are replaced by manufactured and standardized commodities, people become even more desensitized to the very primary components of life that sustain them, such as real food and ordinary plant life, like flowers. No studies are needed to correlate the effects of these conventions on the human spirit, but they do exist and they tell an important story.

During the 1970s, there was a movement in the corrections system known as "prevention and diversion." The idea was to get to parents of youth who were beginning to act out and teach them better parenting skills, hence promoting stronger connections and circumventing deviant behavior. For youth who got into the system, diversion programs focused on group participation in Outward Bound-type programs that fostered connections and collaboration and school interventions that helped kids stay more involved and focused on achieving academic success. The goal was to keep kids from growing into adults who reoffended and ended up in prison. Interaction with nature and working together were the keys to helping young people find their way into adulthood without a criminal record. Those programs lost political favor and, eventually, funding.

We now live in an era where the combination of outdated drug laws, poverty, and the power of prosecutors (in sentencing) have created a pipeline to prisons and prison reformers are turning to these earlier discoveries that worked to help reconnect offenders to themselves and society. Nature and food are a huge component of this, and it has been found that connecting communities with gardens and growing fosters "personal and communal growth by providing a framework within which [they] can participate in a shared experience, interact in an atypical environment, and contribute to a body of shared knowledge."[3]

The same has been true for prisoners and growing food in gardens. As such, prisons are now developing programs that can help inmates restore a sense of connection to themselves, the natural world, and community through growing and tending gardens and producing real food. How can growing vegetables help prisons and inmates? The question seems rhetorical but bears explication in the context of this book. Although it might be tempting to stereotype prison inmates one way or the other as sociopaths or just people who did something illegal and were caught, we don't really know the story of each individual. What we do know is that all human beings have certain needs. The psychologist Abraham Maslow brilliantly illustrated these needs in pyramid form, expressing a hierarchy, the foundation of which is composed of the physiological needs of breathing, food, water, sex, sleep, homeostasis, and excretion.[4] When these needs are satisfied, one can move toward higher goals such as safety, love and belonging, esteem, and self-actualization. What happens when people are cut off from the source of their most primitive needs? More to the point, what happens to inmates when they are reconnected to the source of many of these needs?

Programs such as the Insight Garden Program, Planting Justice, and the Prison Garden Project are being recognized for multiple levels of effectiveness within prisons, even maximum-security prisons such as San Quentin Penitentiary in California, and have even been said to reduce recidivism rates (which is, by and large, the number-one metric upon which success in the corrections arena is judged). An NPR piece on the efforts to enroll inmates in prison garden programs lauded their dramatic successes: "According to the Pew Charitable Trusts, more than four in ten offenders return to prison within three years. By contrast, Planting Justice says the recidivism rate for the men who go through the garden program is 10 percent.

Programs in other states have had similar successes—apparently, gardening behind bars seems to help people steer clear of crime once they get out."[5] On their Web site, the Insight Garden Program (IGP) claims that recidivism rates for participants in their program, which, in addition to gardening also incorporates meditation, emotional process work, and ecotherapy, hover below 10 percent. These measures can save the state a lot of money as prisoners do not return to the system: "[Insight Garden Program] is one of the only evidence-based rehabilitation programs in California. A 2011 recidivism study of 117 IGP participants who paroled between 2003–2009 found that less than 10 percent returned to prison or jail—an approximate savings of $40 million to the state and taxpayers based on the average state cost to incarcerate someone at $47,421."[6] That is a staggering statistic to contend with, and it is particularly crucial in a state like California, which has some of the nation's most overcrowded prisons and jails.

Prison gardens are not a novel idea; they have been used throughout history to cut costs and provide penitentiaries with food using free labor from the inmates. But conceptualizing them as a tool to reduce recidivism, foster community, and give inmates marketable job skills is a more modern conception. Why have they been so successful, and what is it about gardening food in particular that helps reform inmates?

1. Fostering connection to and having responsibility for living things.
2. Access to fresh air and a physical connection to nature.
3. Growing fresh foods that feed themselves and other inmates.
4. Donating fresh foods to shelters and others who need food and developing compassion for others.
5. Working together with others toward a positive goal.
6. Developing skills that can be transferred to a job after prison.

According to NPR, the Planting Justice program, working in conjunction with IGP, hired ten former inmates over a three-year period for landscaping work that paid an entry-level wage of $17.50 per hour.[7]

In a book and guide devoted to the topic entitled *Doing Time in the Garden*, author James Jiler points to the merits of practicing horticulture for inmates in particular:

> Unlike programs in hospitals, drug abuse centers, psychiatric wards, or hospices that target select populations, prison populations encompass a range of personal and mental disorders, physical ailments and anti-social behavior. . . . [So,] horticulture "behind bars" aims to explore the potential of each individual and his/her struggle for change, growth and self-realization. The garden provides an important medium for this dynamic process.[8]

Another positive effect of jail and prison gardens or farms is that they often have a boon of crops—as is the case with any average farm or garden, you will likely at some point just have more rutabagas or squash or pumpkins than you know what to do with. This is true even when you are feeding an inmate population. Many jails and prison food-growing programs often donate their boon to needy families, food banks, or charities when they find themselves with too much produce. This has the doubly important effect of (a) giving prisoners a feeling of contributing back to the greater good and (b) showing the general population that prisoners can make meaningful contributions to the communities they are near. In Pennsylvania, a program called Roots of Re-Entry has donated tens of thousands of pounds of organic produce since the program's inception. One participant of the program said, "It's a beautiful thing to plant something and see it grow. . . . It makes me feel like I'm giving back for some of the things I did wrong."[9] In North Carolina, a similar story on North Carolina Public Radio said that seven prison gardens stock their local food banks with some of the most-needed, hardest-to-find items: fresh produce.[10]

Farm/garden and farm-to-table programs have been implemented at many correctional institutions, sometimes with the help of nonprofit partners and other times as internal initiatives. These include San Diego's Richard J. Donovan Correctional Facility, the Vermont Department of Corrections, Montana Women's Prison, Washington State Department of Corrections, Michigan Department of Corrections, and Oregon State Correctional Institution to name some. Budgets for these programs range anywhere from just $4,000 to $60,000 a year to run, and can include greenhouses (for colder climates).[11] Wehtahna Tucker, program coordinator for the Donovan Correctional Institution program in San Diego told the *Huffington Post* that she feels the program can greatly benefit inmates: "We wanted to create more opportunities for inmates to have a more meaningful experience while they're here, so when they leave, they cannot come back. . . . We want them to be productive while they're incarcerated . . . and show that when they're invested in something, they have something they can look to as an achievement."[12]

While many examples of successful gardening and farming programs exist across the country, not all are without controversy. One of the most famous prison farms sits on a number of acres near one of America's most notorious prisons: Louisiana State Prison, often colloquially known as Angola or even "The Farm," where 80 percent of the inmates are African American.[13] Inmates at Angola participate in many reform programs, including farming large swaths of fields that, for many critics, is far too eerily similar to plantation slave labor of eras past. The warden, Burl Cain, famous for his reforms that made the prison less violent, has a strongly biblical take on rehabilitation that has raised eyebrows as well.[14]

## PRISON CULINARY PROGRAMS

While they are not new, culinary programs in prison are finding new meaning as society moves away from simply trying to fill positions of labor in prisons and begins to see how offering a practical skillset can make viable citizens out of inmates upon their release. Current recidivism rates hover near 60 percent. Considering that nearly 700,000 prisoners are released from prison each year, it is imperative that they are able to reassimilate into communities. This includes enabling them to rejoin (or join) the workforce. As Aaron Taube at *Business Insider* wrote, "It's hard to overstate how important finding a job is for people first coming out of prison. It's a boost of self-confidence, a stabilizing force, and a means of supporting themselves as they work to reenter mainstream society."[15] A Rand Corporation study in 2013 found that inmates who participated in correctional education programs, from remedial education to develop reading and math skills, GED preparation, postsecondary education, or vocational training were 43 percent less likely to return to prison within three years of release compared to those who did not participate in such programs.[16]

There are a variety of programs available, including some "prison restaurants" and culinary training programs that put inmates on a direct path to finding work in the hospitality industry after they are released.

In Concord, Massachusetts, at Northeastern Correctional Center, inmates run a restaurant within the prison walls called Fife and Drum, which has been in operation since 1979. The concept is simple: For about $3, customers can go through security, come in, and eat a full-service hot lunch served up by inmates honing their skills in the kitchen, though the knives are tethered to tables or locked up for supervised use.[17] A review on Chowhound makes the meals sound pretty appealing for the price:

> The food is good, basic food. A large bowl of soup and the salad comes first. It's a beef soup today. A nice clean tasting broth with chunks of beef in it—tastes homemade because the broth has a rich fattiness typical of homemade stock. The salad is a simple bowl of iceberg lettuce with some carrot shreds and a few onion slices. The entrée arrives and it's a big portion of braised boneless short ribs (or chuck) with potatoes and green beans. The beef was rich and tender. For dessert, there's two choices today—chocolate mousse and lemon meringue pie. Unfortunately, they were out of the mousse so I went with the pie. The pie was just okay. It was a graham cracker crust with a mild lemon pudding filling topped with meringue. Overall, the entrée was the best part of the meal.[18]

Perhaps more important than the flavors that come out of the kitchen are the flourishing skills and reacclimation in interacting with the general population that the inmates going through the program receive. A similar program in Milan, Italy (another country suffering from a high recidivism rate) allows inmates to participate in running a restaurant, from front to back located inside the Bollate prison. "It is a matter of pride, a way to make people happy and show them that even inmates can change and evolve," one inmate told the *New York Times* in an interview.[19]

Other successful programs receive inmates when they exit prison. Homeboy Industries, based in Los Angeles, helps former gang members and the formerly incarcerated reacclimate to life on the outside. Their programs include social enterprises with a bakery, catering services, a diner at City Hall, and a café in LAX airport, all run by those enrolled in their programs. As their Web site states, their mission is to change the course of these folks' lives: "When some trainees come to Homeboy, they have never left their neighborhoods, except to go to prison. Here, the world opens up to them—whether they enroll in college, get a driver's license, or accompany Fr. Greg on one of his many speaking engagements around the world, trainees begin to travel, both literally and metaphorically."[20]

## THE ROLE OF HIGHER EDUCATION

Building awareness through education is another extension of the prison garden movement. Portland State University currently offers a capstone course to students, called "Women's Prison Gardens" at a nearby prison. Course objectives are as follows:

> Develop an understanding of the impact of the incarceration of women on individuals, families, communities and the environment. Develop an understanding of the diversity of individuals in correctional facilities; bring some humanity to the idea of "prisoner." Work collaboratively with fellow students, inmates and Department of Corrections employees. Develop a model for a prison garden program that addresses the unique needs of women inmates. Engage in work that is meaningful and become an agent of change by making contributions that impact individuals and communities. Create a presentation that communicates the proposed garden program model and its potential impact.[21]

How can an approach like this help? Courses like this, where students and inmates interact, help each person involved connect the conceptual to real life experience. Students who engage in community service or service learning projects often bring the seeds of change forward through further engagement. One might speculate that alliances and partnerships made at this local level have the capacity to lead to progressive policy changes that can positively impact the lives of those on the "inside" and the "outside." Prison gardens can be a change agent that can help pull us out of the medieval concept of punishment toward progressive reform.

In the case of this course, aspects that stand out are understanding the unique needs of women inmates and bringing some humanity to the idea of "prisoner." Many women who offend and are incarcerated have a history of trauma. Many are mothers and many have a history of drug abuse. Emerging theories in the field of recovery from alcohol and drug abuse point toward identifying and healing trauma. The prison garden experience, again, is one of reconnecting with life's most basic needs and can contribute to building a positive self-image through participating in healthy activities. Alongside access to education, yoga, and meditation (e.g., the Prison Mindfulness Initiative www.prisonmindfulnessinitiative.org/), women inmates (as well as men) can have healthy experiences while serving their time.

## PRISONS ABROAD: NORWAY AND WESTERN EUROPE

Whenever we muse about abhorrent American customs or practices, it seems like there is always a Scandinavian example of how to do something much, much better. Whether it's healthcare or furniture or making smoked fish, there seems to be a stellar model of some sort in one of those cold countries in Northern Europe. Prisons are no exception, and while researching some of the best, or most lauded, practices, the example of Norwegian prisons came up quite often.

Norwegian prisons have been heralded in headlines as "radically humane," "superior," and "unbelievably luxurious."[22] These articles have focused on a couple of prisons in Norway that are making dramatic strides in the corrections arena by allowing inmates a lot of autonomy not typically found in other institutions. Norway, it should be noted, is unique in general when it comes to its criminal justice system, particularly compared to the United States: There is no capital punishment (it was banned in 1902) and the maximum sentence, for even the worst offender, is twenty-one years (though a review process can extend this sentence if a prisoner is deemed to not have been rehabilitated).[23] At some point, as noted in almost every article on the matter, a convicted criminal will return to society. Given that these people will one day be back "in the mix," Norway's focus is much more on rehabilitation or "reintegration," and a huge part of their conception of that seems to be allowing a prisoner to feel human and autonomous, as well as empowered to reorient their life to a purpose that is meaningful.[24] The freedoms that these facilities tout include wearing one's own clothes, being able to visit friends and family on the outside, and of course their treatment of food differs.

Inmates in the Norwegian prison of Bastoey are some of the worst offenders in the country but have some of the most liberal rules that prisoners in the world can have. At Bastoey, inmates are allowed to have their own small homes, bungalows of sorts, with TVs, kitchens, furniture, and all the necessary utensils for cooking (including knives).²⁵ They cook their own food, but also just as importantly, they grow much of it themselves. The prisoners are allowed to attend school classes on-site, participate in gardening and animal husbandry on the small farm plot that the prison has, and even do such things as chainsaw down trees in the nearby woods. While these activities are supervised, none of the guards carry guns, and the atmosphere is one of trust versus one of contempt.²⁶ It seems to be working. When *Vice* did a short film documenting the prison, one of the inmates said quite simply "Here it's more normal so you can act more normal when you get out."²⁷

Another Norwegian prison, Halden, has been showcased in the *New York Times* which called it "modern, cheerful and well appointed" and the reporter describes in detail a scene in which inmates make waffles topped with local brown cheese—a Norwegian tradition they do once a week.²⁸ The reporter goes on to describe the foodways at Halden:

> At Halden, some inmates train for cooking certificates in the prison's professional-grade kitchen classroom, where I was treated to chocolate mousse presented in a wineglass, a delicate nest of orange zest curled on top. But most of the kitchen activity is more ordinary. I never entered a cell block without receiving offers of tea or coffee, an essential element of even the most basic Norwegian hospitality, and was always earnestly invited to share meals. The best meal I had in Norway—spicy lasagna, garlic bread and a salad with sun-dried tomatoes—was made by an inmate who had spent almost half of his forty years in prison. "Every time, you make an improvement," he said of his cooking skills.²⁹

It should be noted that many of the prisons in Norway do not reflect this extreme of a model. While they tend toward reintegration and rehabilitative practices, they do not all give freedoms so liberally. In fact, many of the comments I found in response to these articles online were from disgruntled Scandinavians saying that Americans often overly revere all things Scandinavian, and that in fact many of the prisons in their country were more similar to the American model. I dug into this and that does seem to be the case, down to the food, which is not as appalling as the American fare, but certainly not "unbelievably luxurious" (as *Business Insider* called it).³⁰ The *New York Times*, in its piece on Halden, even admitted that American descriptions of Norwegian prisons are often "hyperbolic" in the media.³¹ It may be worth considering also that Americans' conception of prisons is negative, so any time Americans see a hint of normalcy within a penitentiary, they are easily wowed by it. The punishment model has become so ingrained in American culture that the rehabilitation model, in any capacity, shocks and awes us (similar to the way we conceptualize Norwegian healthcare as being totally "free" and "superb").

All of Western Europe (and the world) has a much lower incarceration rate per capita than the United States, though during the 1960s these rates were largely the same.[32] The examples highlighted in recent news often feature institutions focused on getting criminals to reform and assimilate back into society. This is based on a societal mentality that seems to differ from America: Rather than creating socially isolated human beings by punishing them through revocation of all of their basic human rights, including food, prisons in Europe often demonstrate the belief that criminals can and should reform. European prisons understand that prisoners will one day reenter society, and prepare them as such. In Germany, the overarching principle is "therapy over security."[33]

# 8

# Last Meals

There are only three ways out of prison: release, escape, and death. When Dana Bowerman was released from prison at the end of 2015 after serving over thirteen years for a nonviolent drug offense, she spoke to NPR about the first breakfast she had been able to choose for herself in more than a decade: "I had five pieces of different kinds of pizza," Bowerman told *All Things Considered* in an interview. "Been waiting fifteen years for that. I about choked though because I got kind of emotional and I'd have a mouthful of pizza . . . and it still feels very surreal."[1] Bowerman's experience is typical of the majority of inmates, with almost ten thousand former offenders released back into society each week, according to the Department of Justice Web site.[2] For them, their last meal in prison is not the final meal of their life. But for a small portion of inmates, those that are sentenced to be executed by the state they live in and the laws that govern it, a final meal is made by the prison kitchen.

## THEORIES ON LAST MEALS

Last meals are the stuff of legend and public fascination. What men and women request for a final meal reflects their past as well as how they are choosing to face their death. Since food universalizes us as human beings, last meal requests often tug at the heartstrings of those following inmate stories in the media. Since a brief moratorium on the death penalty between 1972 and 1976, capital punishment by states has been federally reinstated and is currently used in thirty-four of the fifty states, with a total of around 1,400 executions taking place since the reinstatement in 1988.[3] The most significant year for capital punishment in recent history was 1999 in which a record ninety-eight people were executed.[4] In 2013, the United States executed thirty-nine people. In 2014, the number executed was thirty-five, and in 2015, there were twenty-eight executions under capital punishment laws. While the debate rages on as to whether this form of punishment should be part of a society in the modern world, it persists.

A fascinating component of prison food has to do with this set of prisoners: death row inmates. Death row is not only a state of being, but a separate prison block— think *Silence of the Lambs* when Jodie Foster's character Clarice visits Anthony Hopkins's convicted serial killer character Hannibal for the first time.

Boston Marathon Bomber Dzhokhar Tsarnaev is said to have been sent to Terre Haute, Indiana, a notorious prison facility that has been, over the years, specifically designed to house the most dangerous inmates that have been given the death penalty. The death row section of the prison is deliberately isolating, and convicted inmates sit solitarily contemplating their fate. Terre Haute is described below:

> The maximum-security prison contains a special confinement unit where death row inmates are housed. Cells in the unit contain a shower, a desk, a locker, a toilet, a sink and a 13-inch color television. Inmates in the unit are confined to their cells most of the day. They are allowed five hours of outside recreation per week. They are also given the opportunity to use the prison's law library and to participate in religious activities. Tsarnaev's communication with the outside world will be severely restricted to only immediate family members and others approved by the federal government.[5]

Though they eat the regular prison fare alone in their cells, delivered through the chute, often for years while waiting for execution day, inmates are still offered the ritual of being given the choice of what they would like to consume for their last meal. This, along with a final speech are, according to history professor Daniel LaChance, an "arbitrary" but traditional, and even perhaps necessary, component to keeping the public from being outraged at the practice of the death penalty in general. Last meals fascinate the public:

> offenders' last words, last meal requests, and their subsequent broadcast to the public may permit a sympathetic identification with offenders and weaken portrayals of them as irredeemable figures unworthy of sympathy or rehabilitation. Eating and coming to terms with death are two tasks—one mundane, the other existential—that observers will inevitably share with those executed.[6]

The public is furthermore fascinated with death row and, more specifically, last meals and last meal requests because, as Hannah Goldfield points out in her *New*

*Yorker* article on a group of Londoners catching flack after staging a pop-up dinner based on last meal requests: "We're captivated by our most gruesome criminals, and so we want to know everything about them, down to what they most liked to eat. To be reminded, perhaps, of their utter ordinariness and humanity, which makes their unimaginably transgressive acts all the more thrilling."[7]

What can last meals tell us about prisoners, public perception of criminals, and our foodways? It turns out, a lot. Can they even tell innocence or, at least, self-perceived innocence? Researchers at Cornell University's Food Lab studied last meals extensively and, in one study, aimed to see if the amount of calories requested correlated to perceived innocence by inmates. The particular questions were if a criminal who has accepted guilt (confessed) is more likely to indulge in a last meal and if there were any differences between the orders of confessors versus those who maintained their innocence. Their findings were fascinating:

> After analyzing the last meals of 247 people who were executed in the United States between 2002 and 2006, [researchers] found the hypothesis [that those who perceived themselves as innocent would request fewer calories or decline a last meal] to be accurate. Those who denied guilt were 2.7 times more likely to decline a last meal than those who admitted guilt. Furthermore, those who were admittedly guilty requested 34 percent more calories of food and were more likely to request brand name, comfort-food items.[8]

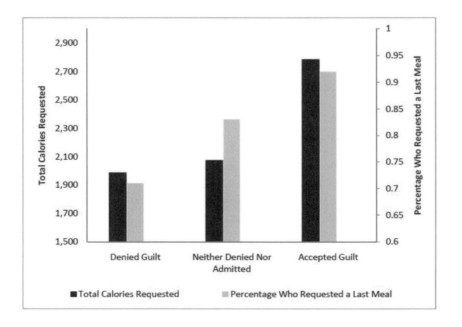

## CAN A DEATH ROW PRISONER ORDER ANYTHING (AND GET IT)?

Societally, we generally have some presumptions about last meals, and fantastical stories have been concocted surrounding them. Often when people think about last meals, we think that prisoners can have the most decadent and wildly imagined dish possible. Or that they are able to order their favorite dish from any menu in any restaurant far and wide, and that these requests will be accommodated. In a word, maybe we seem to believe (or want to believe) that there is a final moment of dignity given to these prisoners. Information about their last meals invites speculation, as LaChance articulates, "[The requests] invite us to contemplate personality, to perceive gluttony, and fearlessness, ascetic restraint and fearfulness among orders for T-Bone steaks and ice cream."[9] And, it would also seem that there is a bit of presumption about the level of taste involved—one assumes that all inmates choose something at least akin to lobster and filet mignon for their final meal.

There are two major myths to debunk here, however: One is that while prisoners may be able to *request* what the most decadent side of their mind can imagine, these elaborate demands often go unfulfilled. I think we often take solace in thinking that at least these prisoners get one final meal of their choosing—whatever their imagination can come up with. The truth is, however, that the person preparing the meal is not some exceptional chef the facility has brought in from the fanciest local restaurant (and, often these federal correctional institutions are really in the middle of nowhere); rather the cook is the "head chef" of the correction facility. Additionally, the requests are often cobbled together from whatever the typical menu rotation for the week or month offers. According a *Slate* article on the topic:

> Final meals are generally limited to food that can be prepared on-site. Virginia prisons have a twenty-eight-day rotating menu—for example, hot dogs on the first day of the cycle, chili on the second day, etc.—and prisoners facing imminent execution are limited to one of the twenty-eight. Other states are more flexible. In Texas, the chef at the Huntsville unit where executions take place tries to accommodate any order. But sometimes that means cooking a close approximate.[10]

The second perception to debunk is the delusion that these prisoners are allowed a *carte blanche* to get whatever they want. In fact, this could not be farther from the truth. As mentioned, the meals are often composed only of what is already available in the prison cafeteria or commissary, and some states have even nixed last meals altogether. The budget for a last meal hovers around $40 depending on the state. Alcohol is basically never allowed, due to facilities not wanting an incoherent or rowdy prisoner on their hands at the last minute. According to *Slate*, prisoners' last meal requests trickle down to the public through the prison's communications representative, but prisoners can also choose to keep them confidential.[11]

More often than not, last meals go uneaten. In 2011, Texas, which had already pared down last meals to only already-available ingredients, decided to abolish the practice of last meals altogether when inmate Lawrence Russell Brewer requested a particularly elaborate meal composed of:

> a pound of barbecue with half a loaf of white bread; three fajitas "with fixings"; a cheese omelet with "ground beef, tomatoes, onions, bell peppers and jalapenos"; two chicken fried steaks "smothered in gravy with sliced onions"; a "triple meat" bacon cheeseburger with "fixings on the side"; a "large bowl" of fried okra; a "meat lovers" pizza; a pint of vanilla ice cream; a "slab" of peanut butter fudge with crushed peanuts; and three root beers.[12]

He was given some of the items and ended up eating nothing. Because of outrage surrounding the fact that he did not touch any of it, the Texas Department of Criminal Justice banned last meal requests altogether. Death row inmates are now given the same meal as all prisoners on the day of their execution. Oklahoma, which has executed 176 men and three women since 1915 allows death row inmates just $15 to spend on a last meal and that meal must come from a restaurant in the town where the death chamber is. There is a Pizza Hut in the town, so requests for large meat lover's pizzas and soda have been popular.[13]

When it comes to last meals, inmates cannot have whatever they want, and they rely on the prison kitchen to make a close approximate. One volunteer chef, a former inmate who felt called to fulfill as best he could the requests made by death row inmates, told the *New York Times* that he did the best he could with the ingredients on hand:

> And, like if they requested lobster, they'd get a piece of frozen pollock. Just like they would normally get on a Friday, but what I'd do is wash the breading off, cut it diagonally and dip it in a batter so that it looked something like at Long John Silver's—something from the free world, something they thought they were getting, but it wasn't. They quit serving steaks in 1994, so whenever anyone would request a steak, I would do a hamburger steak with brown gravy and grilled onions, you know, stuff like that. The press would get it as they requested it, but I would get their handwritten last meal request about three days ahead of time and I'd take it to my captain and say, "Well, what do you want me to do?" And she'd lay it out for me. I tried to do the best I could with what I had.[14]

## TRENDS IN LAST MEALS

A hugely fascinating indicator that came out of researching last meals, not only about prisoners or criminals, but also about our current American industrio-food-complex, is often the simplicity of some of the requests. One inmate, who was known to have managed a Kentucky Fried Chicken for three years, requested a bucket of their Original Recipe chicken, indicating not only a desire for what we commonly call comfort food, but comfort food with a huge twinge of nostalgia for his particular past.[15]

Fast food makes an appearance on many last meal menus. The tendency seems to be for the familiar or the comforting, rather than the extravagant. For Americans, especially those having grown up in low-income households, fast food is a staple, a familiar face, a consistent and reliable distractor whose flavors do not waiver. When it comes down to it, that familiarity and nostalgia are probably precisely the feelings that one desires, almost akin to an old friend.

Another study from the Cornell University Food Lab looked at 247 last meals between 2000 and 2006 to see what meal choices were like "when the future holds no value" and what they found was an impressive amount of similar themes across last meals:

Frequency of Popular Foods Requested for Last Meals (n = 193).

| | | Number of Meals | Percentage of Meals |
|---|---|---|---|
| **Meat** | | | |
| | Chicken | 72 | 37.3% |
| | Hamburger | 46 | 23.8% |
| | Steak | 42 | 21.8% |
| | Pork/Bacon | 34 | 17.3% |
| | Fish/Seafood | 17 | 8.8% |
| **Vegetables** | | | |
| | Salad | 52 | 26.9% |
| | Coleslaw | 13 | 6.7% |
| **Fruits** | | | |
| | Bananas | 4 | 2.1% |
| | Strawberries | 2 | 1.6% |
| | Apple | 1 | .4% |
| **Starches** | | | |
| | French fries | 79 | 40.9% |
| | Other potato | 40 | 20.7% |
| | Bread | 33 | 17.1% |
| | Rice | 3 | 1.6% |
| | Pasta | 3 | 1.6% |
| **Dairy** | | | |
| | Milk | 22 | 11.4% |
| **Drinks** | | | |
| | Soft Drinks | 108 | 60.0% |
| | Milk | 22 | 11.4% |
| | Tea/Coffee | 17 | 8.8% |
| | Juice | 11 | 5.7% |
| **Desserts** | | | |
| | Ice Cream | 47 | 24.3% |
| | Pie | 46 | 23.8% |
| | Cake | 31 | 16.1% |

Researchers found that the food choices were consistent with previous findings when people were experiencing feelings of stress and distress . . . [and] the most commonly requested foods were also calorically dense being meat (83.9%), fried chicken (67.9%), desserts (66.3%), and soft drinks (60%). Requests for specific brands were also common, occurring in 39.9% of meals. Finally, 20% of the sample opted to eat nothing.[16]

Additionally, the study found that the last meal is categorically rich (averaging 2,756 calories) and high in protein. Fast food and brand name beverages were also prominent in the requests. As mentioned in the first chapter, those that are imprisoned are typically our nation's least well off citizens, and the findings of the Cornell study reaffirm that the choices for last meals made by inmates on death row reflect that. "Fruits and vegetables were not often on these individuals' wish list. This pattern of meals shows a preference for foods associated with resource-poor environments with food insecurity."[17] See the charts below for compilations found in the study.

**39.9% Requested Brand Name Foods and Beverages**

**(n= 193)**

|  | Number of Meals | Percentage of Meals |
|---|---|---|
| **Beverages** | | |
| **Coke** | 31 | 16.0% |
| **Pepsi** | 15 | 7.7% |
| **Dr. Pepper** | 14 | 7.3% |
| **Diet Coke** | 3 | 1.6% |
| **Fast Foods** | | |
| **McDonalds** | 3 | 1.6% |
| **KFC** | 3 | 1.6% |
| **Wendy's** | 2 | 1.0% |

## NOTORIOUS LAST MEALS

There have been many notorious last meals throughout history. They can be notorious for many reasons, such as for the meal itself, for the fact that the inmate requesting it is himself or herself notorious, or because the request was outright bizarre.

Karla Faye Tucker, known as the "Pickax Murderer," was the first woman to be executed in the state of Texas since 1863 and the second in Texas history, when she was given a lethal injection in 1998.[18] Tucker sat on death row in Texas for over fourteen years while her case went through numerous appeals. During her time in prison, Tucker underwent an overwhelming and overt religious conversion to Christianity, which garnered her some sympathy from the Christian Right but was not enough to change President George W. Bush's (at the time Texas's governor) final word on her execution.[19] When she was executed on February 3, 1998, "For her last meal, she requested a banana, a peach and a salad, with either Ranch or Italian dressing. Tucker also chose to be executed wearing the white prison uniform that has been her only wardrobe for more than fourteen years."[20] Such a fresh, no frills choice all around. Was this last meal (and her garb), in its simplicity and cleanliness, maybe an unsuccessful final plea for her piety and purity?

Other inmates use their meal requests as a way to convey political and religious beliefs or to demonstrate social consciousness. Odell Barnes, Jr., ordered helpings of "Justice, Equality, World Peace." Jonathan Nobles asked for the Eucharist. Carlos Santana asked for "Justice, Temperance, with Mercy." Danny Harris wanted "God's saving grace, love, truth, peace, and freedom."[21]

Other prisoners go for volume. Peter J. Miniel, for example, requested twenty beef tacos, twenty beef enchiladas, two double cheeseburgers, a pizza with jalapeños, fried chicken, spaghetti with salt, a small fruit cake, half of a chocolate cake, half of a vanilla cake, cookies-n-cream ice cream, caramel pecan fudge ice cream, two Coca-Colas, two Pepsi-Colas, two root beers, and two orange juices.

### Timothy McVeigh

Victor Feguer was the last execution before the United States' thirty-eight-year hiatus of federal executions before the death of Oklahoma City Bomber Timothy McVeigh who killed 168 people in a mass-murder plot. During this hiatus in federally administered executions, the United States was grappling with the notion of capital punishment, how best to carry them out (after some awful fumbles), and took pause to examine why a disproportionate number of nonwhites were being executed.[22] When it came time for McVeigh to request a last meal for his execution by lethal injection, he, like Feguer, had a terribly simple and somewhat befuddling request: Two pints of mint chocolate chip ice cream. The brand? Ben & Jerry's.[23]

### Phillip Ray Workman

When death row inmate Phillip Ray Workman requested that his last meal, a vegetarian pizza, be given to a homeless person in lieu of him having a last meal, his request was denied and Workman refused to eat. When word got out around Nashville, Tennessee, near where he was incarcerated, the community began to rally to honor his request, buying over 150 pizzas and donating them to a local food shelf for distribution to the homeless.[24] When word spread beyond the local news stations to national media, pizza orders trickled in from all over the country.

### John Wayne Gacy

Gacy, the "Killer Clown," one of America's most notorious serial killers, who murdered over thirty young men, requested an elaborate final meal before his lethal injection. The meal request consisted of a dozen fried shrimp, a bucket of Kentucky Fried Chicken Original Recipe chicken, French fries, and one pound of strawberries. As a young man, Gacy had managed a Kentucky Fried Chicken restaurant in the late 1960s. His final words were "Kiss my ass."[25]

### Ronnie Lee Gardner

It may shock you to know that in Utah in 2010, a man was executed by firing squad. Gardner, a convicted murderer, requested what is in my mind a very classic last meal of steak, a lobster tail, apple pie, and vanilla ice cream, but the kicker is that he wanted to eat it while watching the Lord of the Rings trilogy.[26]

### Thomas J. Grasso

Thomas J. Grasso requested:

> Two dozen steamed mussels, two dozen steamed clams, a double cheeseburger from Burger King, half-dozen barbecue spare ribs, two strawberry milkshakes, half a pumpkin pie with whipped cream with diced strawberries, and a 16-ounce can of spaghetti with meatballs, served at room temperature. He later complained "I did not get my SpaghettiOs, I got [canned] spaghetti. I want the press to know this.[27]

### Robert Lee Willie

Willie was a death row prisoner in Louisiana, convicted of rape and murder. Willie was famously portrayed by the actor Sean Penn in the 1995 film *Dead Man Walking*, which brought national attention to the death penalty in the 1990s. Before he was strapped to the electric chair, he told the victim's family that he hoped they got relief from his death. Earlier that evening, he had requested and eaten a last meal of fried fish, oysters, shrimp, fries, and a salad.[28]

## Ricky Ray Rector

Rector, a convicted murderer who was executed on January 24, 1992, requested that his last meal consist of fried chicken, steak, cherry Kool Aid, and a pecan pie. When he left the pie and didn't eat it, he famously told one of the prison guards he was "saving it for later."[29]

## Joseph Mitchell Parsons

Three Burger King Whoppers, two large orders of fries, a chocolate shake, chocolate chip ice cream, and a package of grape Hubba Bubba bubblegum, to be shared with his brother and a cousin.[30]

## Victor Feguer

Perhaps the most haunting last meal I came across in my research was that of Victor Feguer. Feguer was the last person ever to be executed by hanging in the State of Iowa and was the last person to be executed for thirty-eight years before Timothy McVeigh in 2001. He had committed the "brutally random" murder of a doctor named Edward Bartels, and was executed on March 15, 1963. Feguer's story is puzzling, because he was deemed mentally ill, at minimum paranoid schizophrenic, but never spoke about his life, the murder, or the circumstances that led him to commit it.[31] He did not resist authorities or give them trouble, but he did not talk. Feguer prepared for his execution by receiving two new suits—one for the execution and one for his burial.[32] When it came time to ask for his last meal, Feguer requested one of the strangest and simplest last items of food possible: A single olive with the pit still in it.[33] It is rumored that Feguer was buried with the pit.

# Notes

## CHAPTER 1

1. Danielle Kaeble, Lauren Glaze, Anastasios Tsoutis, and Todd Minton, *Bureau of Justice Statistics: Correctional Populations in the United States, 2014*. Report no. NCJ 249513. January 21, 2016. www.bjs.gov/content/pub/pdf/cpus14.pdf.

2. "The Prison Crisis," American Civil Liberties Union. Accessed May 20, 2015. www.aclu.org/prison-crisis.

3. "Incarceration," The Sentencing Project. Accessed February 10, 2015. www.sentencingproject.org/issues/incarceration/.

4. "Recidivism," National Institute of Justice. Accessed May 20, 2015. www.nij.gov/topics/corrections/recidivism/pages/welcome.aspx.

5. *Bureau of Justice Statistics: Prisoners in 2014*. Report no. NCJ 248955. www.bjs.gov/content/pub/pdf/p14_Summary.pdf.

6. "Highest to Lowest—Prison Population Total," World Prison Brief. Accessed May 14, 2015. www.prisonstudies.org/highest-to-lowest/prison-population-total.

7. Lauren Glaze and Danielle Kaeble, *Correctional Populations in the United States, 2013*. Report no. NCJ 248479. December 2014. www.bjs.gov/content/pub/pdf/cpus13.pdf.

8. Maurice Chammah, "Prison without Punishment." *The Marshall Project*. September 25, 2015. www.themarshallproject.org/2015/09/25/prison-without-punishment#.vAz2hBHXh.

9. "U.S. Prison Population Declined for Third Consecutive Year during 2012." News release, July 25, 2013. Bureau of Justice Statistics. www.bjs.gov/content/pub/press/p12acpr.cfm.

10. "Incarceration," The Sentencing Project.

11. Dorothy E. Roberts, "The Social and Moral Cost of Mass Incarceration in African American Communities," *Stanford Law Review* 56, no. 5 (April 2004): 1275. www.jstor.org/stable/40040178.

12. "Incarceration," The Sentencing Project.

13. Eric Schlosser, "The Prison-Industrial Complex," *The Atlantic*, December 1998.

14. Schlosser, "The Prison-Industrial Complex."

15. *Bureau of Justice Statistics: Prisoners in 2014*. Report no. NCJ 248955.

16. "Racial Disparities in Criminal Justice," American Civil Liberties Union. Accessed July 13, 2015. www.aclu.org/issues/mass-incarceration/racial-disparities-criminal-justice.

17. *The Drug War, Mass Incarceration and Race*, Report. 2015. www.drugpolicy.org/resource/drug-war-mass-incarceration-and-race.

18. Adam Gopnik, "The Caging of America: Why Do We Lock Up so Many People?" *The New Yorker*. January 30, 2012. www.newyorker.com/magazine/2012/01/30/the-caging -of-america.

19. Gopnik, "The Caging of America."

20. Gopnik, "The Caging of America."

21. Michelle Alexander and Cornel West, *The New Jim Crow: Mass Incarceration in the Age of Colorblindness* (New York: New Press, 2012). 1–2.

22. Sonja B. Starr and M. Marit Rehavi. "Mandatory Sentencing and Racial Disparity: Assessing the Role of Prosecutors and the Effects of Booker," *Yale Law Journal*, 2nd ser., 123, no. 1 (October 2013). Accessed July 2, 2015. www.yalelawjournal.org/article/mandatory -sentencing-and-racial-disparity-assessing-the-role-of-prosecutors-and-the-effects-of-booker.

23. Kristin Wartman, "Why Food Belongs in Our Discussions of Race," *Civil Eats*. September 3, 2015. civileats.com/2015/09/03/why-food-belongs-in-our-discussions-of-race/.

24. Wartman, "Why Food Belongs in Our Discussions of Race."

25. Roberts, "The Social and Moral Cost of Mass Incarceration in African American Communities," 1275.

26. Rebecca Godderis, "Food for Thought: An Analysis of Power and Identity in Prison Food Narratives," *Berkeley Journal of Sociology* 50 (2006). www.jstor.org/stable/41035612. 61.

27. Carla Amurao, "Fact Sheet: How Bad Is the School-to-Prison Pipeline?" PBS. March 26, 2013. www.pbs.org/wnet/tavissmiley/tsr/education-under-arrest/school-to-prison-pipeline -fact-sheet/.

28. Marion Nestle, *Food Politics: How the Food Industry Influences Nutrition and Health* (Berkeley: University of California Press, 2007). 31–51.

29. Marion Nestle, "Good News: Obesity Rates Leveling Off. But How Come?" *Food Politics*. January 22, 2012. www.foodpolitics.com/2012/01/good-news-obesity-rates-leveling -off-how-come/.

30. "Personal Correspondence." Letter to the author. April 29, 2010.

31. Diana Fishbein and Susan Pease, "The Effects of Diet on Behavior: Implications for Criminology and Corrections," *Research in Corrections* 1, no. 2 (June 1988). Accessed July 7, 2016. static.nicic.gov/Library/006777.pdf.

32. Ronette R. Briefel, Mary Kay Crepinsek, Charlotte Cabili, Ander Wilson, and Philip M. Gleason, "School Food Environments and Practices Affect Dietary Behaviors of US Public School Children," *Journal of the American Dietetic Association* 109, no. 2 (2009).

33. C. B. Gesch, "Influence of Supplementary Vitamins, Minerals and Essential Fatty Acids on the Antisocial Behaviour of Young Adult Prisoners: Randomised, Placebo-controlled Trial," *British Journal of Psychiatry* 181, no. 1 (2002): 22–28.

34. Bryan Finoki, "Food for Thinkers: WANTED! Prison Food Writers." *GOOD Magazine*. January 31, 2011. Accessed February 11, 2016. www.good.is/articles/food-for-thinkers -wanted-prison-food-writers.

35. Antonio Negri, *The Savage Anomaly: The Power of Spinoza's Metaphysics and Politics* (Minneapolis: University of Minnesota Press, 1991). xxii.

## CHAPTER 2

1. Arthur Griffiths, *Memorials of Millbank, and Chapters in Prison History* (London: Chapman and Hall, 1884). 48.

2. Harry Elmer Barnes, "Historical Origin of the Prison System in America," *Journal of Criminal Law and Criminology* 12, no. 1 (1921). 35–60.

3. Margery Bassett, "The Fleet Prison in the Middle Ages," *University of Toronto Law Journal* 5, no. 2 (1944): 383.

4. Maria Cross and Barbara MacDonald, *Nutrition in Institutions* (Chichester, West Sussex: Wiley-Blackwell, 2009). 279.

5. Bassett, "The Fleet Prison in the Middle Ages," 400.

6. Bassett, "The Fleet Prison in the Middle Ages," 239.

7. Bassett, "The Fleet Prison in the Middle Ages," 399.

8. Bassett, "The Fleet Prison in the Middle Ages," 240.

9. R. B. Pugh, *Imprisonment in Medieval England* (London: Cambridge University Press, 1968). 176.

10. Here we can look to Saumuel K. Cohn's review of Guy Geltner's new book, *The Medieval Prison*, which argues that Italian prisons of the day were actually quite hospitable. It is also noted in Bassett's article on Fleet Prison that American prisons were less harsh, offering prisoners daily meals. S. K. Cohn, "The Medieval Prison: A Social History," *English Historical Review* CXXV, no. 512 (2010): 153–55.

11. Bassett, "The Fleet Prison in the Middle Ages," 399.

12. Bassett, "The Fleet Prison in the Middle Ages," 399.

13. Cross and MacDonald, *Nutrition in Institutions*, 277.

14. Cross and MacDonald, *Nutrition in Institutions*, 278.

15. With Bentham's design, all the prisoners in a prison could be observed by one guard from a specific vantage point in the center of the prison. See: Anne Brunon-Ernst, *Beyond Foucault: New Perspectives on Bentham's Panopticon* (Farnham: Ashgate, 2012).

16. "John Howard (1726–1790)." BBC. Accessed June 12, 2015. www.bbc.co.uk/history/ historic_figures/howard_john.shtml.

17. John Howard, *The State of the Prisons in England and Wales* (Cambridge University Press, 2013). 5–33.

18. Cross and MacDonald, *Nutrition in Institutions*, 280.

19. Cross and MacDonald, *Nutrition in Institutions*, 281.

20. Barnes, "Historical Origin of the Prison System in America," 35–60.

21. Barnes, "Historical Origin of the Prison System in America," 35–60.

22. Barnes, "Historical Origin of the Prison System in America," 35–60.

23. Christina Sterbenz, "The Modern Prison System Was Created in Benjamin Franklin's Living Room," *Business Insider*. April 19, 2015. www.businessinsider.com/the-worlds-first -prison-was-created-in-benjamin-franklins-living-room-2015-3.

24. Barnes, "Historical Origin of the Prison System in America," 35–60.

25. Barnes, "Historical Origin of the Prison System in America," 35–60.

26. Oscar Wilde, *The Ballad of Reading Gaol* (New York: E.P. Dutton, 1928). 37.

27. Cross and MacDonald, *Nutrition in Institutions*, 282.

28. Cross and MacDonald, *Nutrition in Institutions*, 283.

29. Alice Ross, "Health and Diet in 19th-century America: A Food Historian's Point of View," *Historical Archaeology* 27, no. 2 (1993): 42–56.

30. Specifically, we can look to Edward Smith, who, in the mid-1850s did many prison dietary studies that questioned why diet was varied due to length of punishment, why specific

foods were introduced and taken away, how certain foods affected disease outbreaks and how important protein is to hard labor. See: Kenneth J. Carpenter, "Nutritional Studies in Victorian Prisons," *Journal of Nutrition* 136, no. 1 (January 2006): 1–8.

31. Here, we can look to a visiting justice at the model prison at Reading, who is quoted as saying, "If they wished imprisonment to deter from crime, they must cease to supply an excessive diet as to afford temptation to a poor man to commit crime in order to get into prison." J. C. Drummond, Anne Wilbraham, and Dorothy Hollingsworth, *The Englishman's Food: A History of Five Centuries of English Diet* (London: Pimlico, 1957). Quoted in: Cross and MacDonald, *Nutrition in Institutions*, 282.

32. Michel Foucault, *Discipline and Punish: The Birth of the Prison* (New York: Vintage Books, 1995). 83.

33. Cross and MacDonald, *Nutrition in Institutions*, 283.

34. Carpenter, "Nutritional Studies in Victorian Prisons," 1–8.

35. Carpenter, "Nutritional Studies in Victorian Prisons," 1–8.

36. David Cooper and Philip Priestly. "Victorian Prison Lives: English Prison Biography, 1830–1914." *American Historical Review* 91, no. 5 (1986): 1196.

37. "A Taste of Lobster History." History.com. Accessed October 11, 2015. www.history.com/news/a-taste-of-lobster-history.

38. Elisabeth Townsend, *Lobster: A Global History* (London: Reaktion Books, 2011). 34.

39. Mary Bosworth, *Encyclopedia of Prisons and Correctional Facilities* (Thousand Oaks, CA: Sage Publications, 2005). 330.

40. Franz Kafka and Joachim Neugroschel, *The Metamorphosis, In the Penal Colony, and Other Stories: With Two New Stories* (New York: Scribner Paperback Fiction, 2000). 205.

41. Cross and MacDonald, *Nutrition in Institutions*, 289.

42. Cross and MacDonald, *Nutrition in Institutions*, 289.

43. Cross and MacDonald, *Nutrition in Institutions*, 290.

44. Cross and MacDonald, *Nutrition in Institutions*, 290.

45. Cross and MacDonald, *Nutrition in Institutions*, 291.

46. Cross and MacDonald, *Nutrition in Institutions*, 293.

47. Bosworth, *Encyclopedia of Prisons and Correctional Facilities*, 330.

## CHAPTER 3

1. "School Meal Trends and Stats," SchoolNutrition.org. Accessed June 11, 2015. schoolnutrition.org/AboutSchoolMeals/SchoolMealTrendsStats/.

2. Joyce Chediac, "Punishment for Profit: The Economics of Mass Incarceration," Workers World, 2015. www.workers.org/articles/2015/05/04/punishment-for-profit-the-economics-of-mass-incarceration/.

3. Marc Santora, "City's Annual Cost per Inmate Is $168,000, Study Finds," *New York Times*, 2013. www.nytimes.com/2013/08/24/nyregion/citys-annual-cost-per-inmate-is-nearly-168000-study-says.html.

4. Diane Orson, "'Million-Dollar Blocks' Map Incarceration's Costs," NPR, October 2, 2012. www.npr.org/2012/10/02/162149431/million-dollar-blocks-map-incarcerations-costs.

5. Christian Henrichson and Ruth Delaney, *The Price of Prisons: What Incarceration Costs Taxpayers*, Report, July 20, 2012. www.vera.org/sites/default/files/resources/downloads/price-of-prisons-updated-version-021914.pdf.

6. Ta-Nehisi Coates, "The Black Family in the Age of Mass Incarceration," *Atlantic*, October 2015. www.theatlantic.com/magazine/archive/2015/10/the-black-family-in-the-age-of-mass-incarceration/403246/.

7. Jennifer Warren, "For 14 Years, Inmates Have Been Fed for $2.45 a Day," *Los Angeles Times*, June 17, 2002. articles.latimes.com/2002/jun/17/local/me-confood17.

8. "Daily Cost to Feed Prisoners and the Average American," Prison Policy Initiative. Accessed May 24, 2015. www.prisonpolicy.org/graphs/foodcosts.html.

9. Donovan W. Wilson, "Prison Food: Not Fancy, But—," *New York Times*, 1982. www.nytimes.com/1982/12/19/nyregion/prison-food-not-fancy-but.html.

10. Jennifer Waite, "Prison Food: What Are America's Inmates Eating?" *Inmate Aid*, April 9, 2009. www.inmateaid.com/pages/details/prison-food-what-are-americas-inmates-eating-yahoo.

11. Samantha Olson, "I Ate Like a Prisoner for a Week—Here's What Happened," *Medical Daily*, April 27, 2015. Accessed October 11, 2015. www.medicaldaily.com/1-week-prison-food-diet-reveals-problems-inmate-meals-low-cost-bad-taste-and-very-349572.

12. Cara Bruce, "Private Prisons: Lowering the Bar to Turn a Buck?" *Young Money*. Accessed March 8, 2016. finance.youngmoney.com/credit_debt/private-prisons-lowering-the-bar-to-turn-a-buck/.

13. Tracy F. H. Chang and Douglas E. Thompkins, "Corporations Go to Prisons: The Expansion of Corporate Power in the Correctional Industry," *Labor Studies Journal* 27, no. 1 (2002): 45–69. Project Muse.

14. Eric Schlosser, "The Prison-Industrial Complex," *Atlantic*, December 1998.

15. Chang and Thompkins. "Corporations Go to Prisons," 45–69.

16. Associated Press, "AP: Private Prisons Profit from Illegal Immigrants," CBSNews, August 2, 2012. www.cbsnews.com/news/ap-private-prisons-profit-from-illegal-immigrants/.

17. *Tampa Bay Times* (Tampa Bay), "Food Fiasco Costs Inmates, Taxpayers," Editorial, May 14, 2008.

18. Waite, "Prison Food."

19. David Reutter, "Appalling Prison and Jail Food Leaves Prisoners Hungry for Justice," *Prison Legal News*, April 5, 2010. www.prisonlegalnews.org/news/2010/apr/15/appalling-prison-and-jail-food-leaves-prisoners-hungry-for-justice/.

20. "About Us–Trinity Services Group," Trinity Services Group. Accessed March 5, 2015. www.trinityservicesgroup.com/trinity-services-group/.

21. "Correctional Facilities Food Services," Aramark. Accessed December 1, 2015. www.aramark.com/industries/business-government/correctional-facilities/food-services.

22. "Correctional Facilities Food Services," Aramark. "Quality and Nutritional Assurance," Trinity Services Group. Accessed March 5, 2015. www.trinityservicesgroup.com/quality-nutritional-assurance/.

23. Paul Egan, "Maggots Prompt Call for Prison Kitchen Inspections," *Detroit Free Press*. Accessed June 24, 2015. www.freep.com/story/news/local/michigan/2015/06/24/bill-targets-aramark-requiring-prison-kitchen-inspections/29210815/.

24. Reutter, "Appalling Prison and Jail Food Leaves Prisoners Hungry for Justice."

25. Reutter, "Appalling Prison and Jail Food Leaves Prisoners Hungry for Justice."

26. Paul Egan, "Aramark Prison Worker Suspected in Attempted Hired Hit," *Detroit Free Press*, September 25, 2014. Accessed March 8, 2016. www.freep.com/story/news/local/michigan/2014/09/25/aramark-worker-investigated-murder-hire-plot/16172713/.

27. Lisa Rein, "Finally, the Government Has Decided to Eliminate Pork—From the Menu in Federal Prisons," *Washington Post*. October 9, 2015, www.washingtonpost.com/news/federal-eye/wp/2015/10/09/finally-the-government-has-decided-to-eliminate-pork-from-the-menu-in-federal-prisons/.

28. Lisa Rein, "After Firestorm, Pork Roast Is Back on the Menu at Federal Prisons," *Washington Post*, October 16, 2015. www.washingtonpost.com/news/federal-eye/wp/2015/10/16/after-firestorm-pork-roast-is-back-on-the-menu-at-federal-prisons/.

29. Reutter, "Appalling Prison and Jail Food Leaves Prisoners Hungry for Justice."

30. Alan Judd, "Jail Food Complaints Highlight Debate over Outsourcing Public Services," *Atlanta Journal-Constitution*, January 1, 2015. www.myajc.com/news/news/public-affairs/jail-food-complaints-highlight-debate-over-outsour/njZh3/.

31. Shannon McCaffrey, "Prison Blues: States Slimming Down Inmate Meals," *November Coalition*, June 5, 2009. www.november.org/stayinfo/breaking09/Prison_Blues_Inmate_Meals.html.

32. Jacob Davidson, "'America's Toughest Sheriff' Takes Meat off Jail Menu," *TIME*, September 27, 2013. newsfeed.time.com/2013/09/27/americas-toughest-sheriff-takes-meat-off-jail-menu/.

33. *New York Times* (New York), "America's Worst Sheriff (Joe Arpaio)," Editorial, December 31, 2008. theboard.blogs.nytimes.com/2008/12/31/americas-worst-sheriff-joe-arpaio/?_r=0.

34. Tim Boyd, "Cruel and Unusual Punishment: Soy Diet for Illinois Prisoners—Weston A. Price." Weston A. Price Foundation. May 1, 2009. www.westonaprice.org/health-topics/cruel-and-unusual-punishment-soy-diet-for-illinois-prisoners/.

35. *Tampa Bay Times* (Tampa Bay). "Food Fiasco Costs Inmates, Taxpayers." Editorial. May 14, 2008.

36. *Tampa Bay Times* (Tampa Bay), "Food Fiasco Costs Inmates, Taxpayers."

37. Kyle Feldscher, "After Aramark Issues, Lawmakers Propose Having Local Health Departments Inspect Prison Kitchens," *Michigan Live*, June 25, 2015. www.mlive.com/lansing-news/index.ssf/2015/06/after_aramark_issues_lawmakers.html.

38. Colleen Curry, "Michigan Is Booting Aramark from Its Prisons, but Not Over Rat-and-Maggot-Tainted Food," *VICE News*, July 14, 2015. news.vice.com/article/michigan-is-booting-aramark-from-its-prisons-but-not-over-rat-and-maggot-tainted-food.

39. Associated Press, "Opponents Press Snyder to Cancel Prison Contract," *Toledo Blade*. July 30, 2014. www.toledoblade.com/State/2014/07/30/Opponents-press-Snyder-to-cancel-prison-contract.html.

40. Stephen Katz, "What It's Like to Eat some of the Worst Prison Food in America," *VICE News*. September 25, 2015. munchies.vice.com/en/articles/what-its-like-to-eat-some-of-the-worst-prison-food-in-america.

41. Vivian Giang, "Inmate Talks to Us Over an Illegal Cell Phone about Working the Jailhouse Black Market." *Business Insider*. July 2, 2012. www.businessinsider.com/prisoner-shares-with-us-a-glimpse-of-the-hustle-behind-bars-2012-6.

42. Giang, "Inmate Talks to Us Over an Illegal Cell Phone about Working the Jailhouse Black Market."

43. Giang, "Inmate Talks to Us Over an Illegal Cell Phone about Working the Jailhouse Black Market."

44. John Adams, "Commissary Day," *Pen America*. 2012. Accessed June 11, 2015. www.pen.org/nonfiction/commissary-day.

45. "Personal Correspondence," Letter to the author, April 29, 2010.

46. Patrick Larmour, "Getting a Hustle: How to Live Like a King Behind Bars." *The Marshall Project*. January 1, 2016. www.themarshallproject.org/2016/01/15/getting-a-hustle-how-to-live-like-a-king-behind-bars#.Af5v8vtAg.

47. Larmour, "Getting a Hustle."

48. Simone Weichselbaum, "This Is Rikers ('They Let You Kiss Twice')." *The Marshall Project*. June 28, 2015. www.themarshallproject.org/2015/06/28/this-is-rikers#.sUxQQvS8N.

49. Waite, "Prison Food."

## CHAPTER 4

1. Daniel Engber, "What Martha Really Ate in Prison," *Slate*, March 3, 2005. Accessed December 11, 2012. www.slate.com/articles/news_and_politics/explainer/2005/03/what_martha_really_ate_in_prison.html.

2. *US Department of Justice Federal Bureau of Prisons Food Service Manual*. Report no. P4700.06.

3. Hardy, Kathy. "Nutrition Services in Correctional Facilities." *Today's Dietitian*. June 2016. Accessed July 7, 2016. www.todaysdietitian.com/newarchives/0616p32.shtml.

4. Jennifer Waite, "Prison Food: What Are America's Inmates Eating?" *Inmate Aid*, April 9, 2009. www.inmateaid.com/pages/details/prison-food-what-are-americas-inmates-eating-yahoo.

5. Pablo Piña, "Pelican Bay (SHU) Photograph, Canteen List and Menu," *Between the Bars* December 1, 2013. betweenthebars.org/posts/14975/pelican-bayshu-photograph-canteen-list-and-menu.

6. *US Department of Justice Federal Bureau of Prisons Food Service Manual*, Report no. P4700.06, September 13, 2011. www.bop.gov/policy/progstat/4700_006.pdf.

7. *US Department of Justice Federal Bureau of Prisons Food Service Manual*, Report no. P4700.06.

8. Cyrus Naim, "Prison Food Law." Master's thesis, Harvard University, 2005. Accessed March 2, 2015. nrs.harvard.edu/urn-3:HUL.InstRepos:8848245.

9. Naim, "Prison Food Law."

10. Naim, "Prison Food Law."

11. "Seeking Accreditation," American Correctional Association. www.aca.org/ACA_Prod_IMIS/ACA_Member/Standards___Accreditation/Seeking_Accreditation/ACA_Member/Standards_and_Accreditation/Seeking_Accreditation_Home.aspx.

12. "Seeking Accreditation," American Correctional Association.

13. Naim, "Prison Food Law."

14. "Office of the Inspector General—A Message from Inspector General Robert A. Barton," Homepage. Accessed October 1, 2015. www.oig.ca.gov/.

15. Naim, "Prison Food Law."

16. Lizette Alvarez, "You Don't Have to Be Jewish to Love a Kosher Prison Meal," *New York Times*, January 20, 2014. Accessed July 15, 2014. www.nytimes.com/2014/01/21/us/you-dont-have-to-be-jewish-to-love-a-kosher-prison-meal.html.

17. Alvarez, "You Don't Have to Be Jewish to Love a Kosher Prison Meal."

18. Naomi Zeveloff, "Not Just Jews Eat Kosher in Prison," *Forward*, April 30, 2012. Accessed July 1, 2014. forward.com/news/155363/not-just-jews-eat-kosher-food-in-prison/.

19. Zeveloff, "Not Just Jews Eat Kosher in Prison."

20. "Religious Land Use and Institutionalized Persons Act," US Department of Justice, August 6, 2015. Accessed April 17, 2016. www.justice.gov/crt/religious-land-use-and-institutionalized-persons-act.

21. Steve Siporin, "The Kosher Con Game: Who's Keeping Kosher in Prison?" *Western Folklore* 74, no. 1 (Winter 2015): 64.

22. Siporin, "The Kosher Con Game," 69.

23. Scott James, "Jail Time Yields a Clash on Vegetarian Meals," *New York Times*. August 4, 2011. Accessed December 28, 2014. www.nytimes.com/2011/08/05/us/05bcjames.html.

24. James, "Jail Time Yields a Clash on Vegetarian Meals."

25. Federal Bureau of Prisons, Department of Justice, *Bureau of Prisons*, April 22, 1996. Accessed October 4, 2014. www.bop.gov/policy/progstat/4761_004.pdf. Program Statement: 4761.04

26. "Top 10 Vegetarian-Friendly Prisons!" PETA Top 10 Vegetarian Friendly Prisons Comments. December 10, 2007. Accessed November 23, 2014. www.peta.org/blog/top-10-vegetarianfriendly-prisons/.

27. Peter Young, "The Strict Vegan Prisoner Playbook," *Vice News*, September 26, 2013. www.vice.com/read/the-strict-vegan-prisoner-playbook.

28. Doran Larson and B. G. Jacobs, *Fourth City: Essays from the Prison in America* (East Lansing: Michigan State University Press, 2013), 105.

29. Christie Thompson, "When Your Insulin Pump Is Contraband," *The Marshall Project*, April 22, 2015. Accessed December 12, 2015. www.themarshallproject.org/2015/04/22/when-your-insulin-pump-is-contraband.

30. Thompson, "When Your Insulin Pump Is Contraband."

31. Federal Bureau of Prisons, Department of Justice, *Management of Diabetes—Federal Bureau of Prisons Clinical Practice Guidelines*. June 2012. Accessed October 10, 2015. www.bop.gov/resources/pdfs/diabetes.pdf.

32. Federal Bureau of Prisons. Department of Justice. Food Service Manual. September 13, 2011. Accessed October 10, 2015. https://www.bop.gov/policy/progstat/4700_006.pdf. Number: P4700.06

33. Pete Brook, "Rarely Seen Images of the Real San Quentin," *The Marshall Project*. February 10, 2016. Accessed March 23, 2016. www.themarshallproject.org/2016/02/10/rarely-seen-images-of-the-real-san-quentin.

34. J. W. Marquart and J. B. Roebuck, "Institutional Control and the Christmas Festival in a Maximum Security Penitentiary," *Journal of Contemporary Ethnography* 15, no. 3–4 (October 1987): 449–73. doi: 10.1177/089124168701500307.

35. "What Foods Do Inmates Eat in Prison?" *Quora*. Accessed March 2, 2015. www.quora.com/What-foods-do-inmates-eat-in-prison.

36. Eric Lach, "Joe Arpaio Brags about Serving Inmates 56 Cent Thanksgiving Dinner," *Talking Points Memo*, November 29, 2013. Accessed May 2, 2014. talkingpointsmemo.com/livewire/joe-arpaio-brags-about-serving-inmates-56-cent-thanksgiving-dinner.

## CHAPTER 5

1. Rebecca Godderis, "Food for Thought: An Analysis of Power and Identity in Prison Food Narratives," *Berkeley Journal of Sociology* 50 (2006). www.jstor.org/stable/41035612. 61–75.

2. T. Ugelvik, "The Hidden Food: Mealtime Resistance and Identity Work in a Norwegian Prison," *Punishment and Society* 13, no. 1 (2011): 47–63.

3. Cyrus Naim, "Prison Food Law." Master's thesis, Harvard University, 2005. Accessed March 2, 2015. nrs.harvard.edu/urn-3:HUL.InstRepos:8848245.

4. "Eighth Amendment," The Free Dictionary—Legal Dictionary. Accessed February 12, 2014. legal-dictionary.thefreedictionary.com/Eighth Amendment.

5. Bernard J. Farber, ed. "Prisoner Diet Legal Issues." *AELE Monthly Law Journal* 2007, no. 7 (July 2007). www.aele.org/law/2007JBJUL/2007-07MLJ301.pdf.

6. Farber, "Prisoner Diet Legal Issues."

7. Farber, "Prisoner Diet Legal Issues."

8. Farber, "Prisoner Diet Legal Issues."

9. Associated Press, "Colorado: Ruling on Prison Food," *New York Times* [New York], April 24, 2009: A12. Accessed March 3, 2015. www.nytimes.com/2009/04/25/us/25brfs-RULINGONPRIS_BRF.html.

10. Associated Press. "Colorado," A12.

11. "Miss Alice Paul on Hunger Strike," *New York Times*, November 7, 1917. Accessed April 10, 2015. query.nytimes.com/mem/archive-free/pdf?res=9A04E7D9123FE433A25754 C0A9679D946696D6CF.

12. "Miss Alice Paul on Hunger Strike."

13. "Miss Alice Paul on Hunger Strike."

14. Anna Reiter, "Alice Paul and Her Fight for Women's Suffrage," *Armstrong Undergraduate Journal of History*. Accessed June 10, 2015. archive.armstrong.edu/Initiatives/ history_journal/history_journal_fearless_radicalism_alice_paul_and_her_fight_for_womens _suf.

15. Judith Ward, *Ambushed* (London: Vermilion, 1993).

16. George J. Annas, "Law and the Life Sciences: Prison Hunger Strikes: Why the Motive Matters," *The Hastings Center Report* 12.6 (1982): 21.

17. James Ridgeway and Jean Cassella, "America's 10 Worst Prisons: Pelican Bay," *Mother Jones*, May 8, 2013. Accessed April 17, 2015. www.motherjones.com/politics/2013/05/10 -worst-prisons-america-pelican-bay.

18. Ridgeway and Cassella, "America's 10 Worst Prisons."

19. Benjamin Wallace-Wells, "The Plot from Solitary," *New York Magazine*. February 26, 2014. Accessed March 17, 2015. nymag.com/news/features/solitary-secure-housing -units-2014-2/.

20. Rory Carroll, "California Inmates Launch Biggest Hunger Strike in State's History," *The Guardian*, 2013. Accessed March 17, 2015. www.theguardian.com/world/2013/jul/09/ california-prisoners-hunger-strike.

21. Wallace-Wells, "The Plot from Solitary."

22. Wallace-Wells, "The Plot from Solitary."

23. Wallace-Wells, "The Plot from Solitary."

24. Wallace-Wells, "The Plot from Solitary."

25. Wallace-Wells, "The Plot from Solitary."

26. Fresh Air, "How 4 Inmates Launched a Statewide Hunger Strike from Solitary," Advertisement, NPR, March 6, 2014. Accessed March 17, 2015. www.npr.org/templates/ transcript/transcript.php?storyId=286794055.

27. Center for Constitutional Rights, "Summary of Settlement Terms in Anti-solitary Confinement Class Action, *Ashker v. Brown*," *San Francisco Bay View*, September 26, 2015. Accessed April 17, 2015. sfbayview.com/2015/09/summary-of-settlement-terms-in-anti -solitary-confinement-class-action-ashker-v-brown/.

28. Center for Constitutional Rights, "Summary of Settlement Terms in Anti-solitary Confinement Class Action, *Ashker v. Brown*."

29. Center for Constitutional Rights, "Summary of Settlement Terms in Anti-solitary Confinement Class Action, *Ashker v. Brown*."

30. Eliza Barclay, "Food as Punishment: Giving U.S. Inmates 'The Loaf' Persists," NPR: The Salt, January 2, 2014. Accessed March 17, 2015. www.npr.org/sections/thesalt/ 2014/01/02/256605441/punishing-inmates-with-the-loaf-persists-in-the-u-s.

31. Justin Elliot, "What Is Nutraloaf, Anyway?" *Mother Jones*. July 2008. Accessed March 17, 2015. www.motherjones.com/politics/2008/07/what-nutraloaf-anyway.

32. Jeff Ruby, "Dining Critic Tries Nutraloaf, the Prison Food for Misbehaving Inmates," *Chicago Magazine*, August 26, 2010. Accessed March 17, 2015. www.chicagomag .com/Chicago-Magazine/September-2010/Dining-Critic-Tries-Nutraloaf-the-Prison-Food-for -Misbehaving-Inmates/.

33. Barclay, "Food as Punishment."

34. Ruby, "Dining Critic Tries Nutraloaf, the Prison Food for Misbehaving Inmates."

35. Barclay, "Food as Punishment."

36. Barclay, "Food as Punishment."

37. Adam Cohen, "Can Food Be Cruel and Unusual Punishment?" *TIME.com*, April 2, 2012. Accessed March 17, 2015. ideas.time.com/2012/04/02/can-food-be-cruel-and-unusual -punishment/.

38. Barclay, "Food as Punishment."

39. Claudia Restrepo, "Is this Prison Food Cruel and Unusual?" *Buzzfeed*, January 12, 2015. Accessed April 12, 2015. www.buzzfeed.com/claudiarestrepo/adults-try-prison-food.

40. Jesse Mckinley, "New York Prisons Take an Unsavory Punishment off the Table," *New York Times*, December 17, 2015. Accessed April 12, 2015. www.nytimes.com/2015/12/18/ nyregion/new-york-prisons-take-an-unsavory-punishment-off-the-table.html?_r=0.

41. Laura Barnhardt, "Loaves Give Rise to Good Behavior," *Baltimore Sun*, March 25, 2002. Accessed May 2, 2014. articles.baltimoresun.com/2002-03-25/news/0203250211_1_ supermax-loaf-lima-bean.

42. "Personal Correspondence," Letter to the author, April 29, 2010.

43. Margaret R. Kohut, *When You Have to Go to Prison: A Complete Guide for You and Your Family* (Ocala, FL: Atlantic Publishing Group, 2011).

44. *Tampa Bay Times* (Tampa Bay), "Food Fiasco Costs Inmates, Taxpayers," Editorial, May 14, 2008.

45. Felicity Lawrence, "Omega-3, Junk Food and the Link between Violence and What We Eat," *Guardian*, October 17, 2006. Accessed May 12, 2015. www.theguardian.com/politics/ 2006/oct/17/prisonsandprobation.ukcrime.

46. Tito David Valdez, Jr, "Prison Chow Time—If It's Prison Food, It All Tastes the Same," *Inmate.com*. Accessed May 17, 2015. www.inmate.com/prison-articles/prison-chow -time.htm.

47. Milo DeVille, "Literature on Lockdown: Chow in Prison," *Missouri Review*, August 1, 2014. Accessed April 17, 2015. www.missourireview.com/tmr-blog/2014/08/literature-on -lockdown-chow-in-prison/.

48. "Food to Blame for Northpoint Prison Riot?" ABC36TV, November 6, 2009. Accessed March 11, 2015. www.youtube.com/watch?v=ruo80t0c-24.

49. "Food to Blame for Northpoint Prison Riot?"

50. David M. Reutter, "Food Problems Contribute to Riot at Kentucky Prison," *Prison Legal News*, April 15, 2010. Accessed May 7, 2015. www.prisonlegalnews.org/news/2010/ apr/15/food-problems-contribute-to-riot-at-kentucky-prison/.

51. "Chilies Aid Sumatra Jail Break," BBC News, August 22, 2006. Accessed May 2, 2015. news.bbc.co.uk/2/hi/asia-pacific/5274924.stm.

52. Blakinger, Keri. "Beyond Shanks: A Look at Lesser-known Prison Weapons." *New York Daily News*. January 25, 2016. Accessed August 24, 2016. http://www.nydailynews .com/news/national/shanks-lesser-known-prison-weapons-article-1.2508679.

## CHAPTER 6

1. Clifton Collins and Gustavo Alvarez, *Prison Ramen: Recipes and Stories from behind Bars* (New York: Workman, 2015).

2. John Adams, "Commissary Day," *Pen America*. 2012. Accessed June 11, 2015. www .pen.org/nonfiction/commissary-day.

3. Adams, "Commissary Day."

4. "Personal Correspondence," Letter to the author, April 29, 2010.

5. Dorothy Maraglino, "Dorothy Maraglino on Prison: Part 1—Prison Writers," *Prison Writers*. Accessed June 21, 2015. www.prisonwriters.com/dorothy-maraglino-on-prison-part-one/.

6. Amy B. Smoyer, "Feeding Relationships: Foodways and Social Networks in a Women's Prison," *Affilia* 30, no. 1 (2014): 26–39. doi: 10.1177/0886109914537490.

7. Smoyer, "Feeding Relationships," 26–39.

8. Adams, "Commissary Day."

9. "Did Lil Wayne Order Kool-Aid in Jail? Oh Yeah!" TMZ, August 16, 2010. Accessed October 2, 2014. www.tmz.com/2010/08/15/lil-wayne-jail-kool-aid-rikers-island-food.

10. Danielle Gusmaroli, "LI-LO LIVES ON JELLY FOR 14 DAYS IN JAIL; Freed Lohan Heads Straight into Rehab Unit," *Daily Record* (Glasgow, Scotland), August 3, 2010. Accessed December 3, 2012. www.highbeam.com/doc/1G1-233367758.html?refid=easy_hf.

11. Daniel Engber, "What Martha Really Ate in Prison," *Slate*. 2005. Accessed December 11, 2012. www.slate.com/articles/news_and_politics/explainer/2005/03/what_martha_really_ate_in_prison.html.

12. Steve Fishman, "Bernie Madoff, Free at Last," *NYMag.com*, June 6, 2010. Accessed June 1, 2015. nymag.com/news/crimelaw/66468/index3.html.

13. Fishman, "Bernie Madoff, Free at Last."

14. Eric Anderson and Jennifer Peros. "Teresa Giudice Writes About 'Orange' Burgers and Fights in Her Prison Diary," *Us Weekly*, July 2, 2015. Accessed September 12, 2015. www.usmagazine.com/celebrity-news/news/teresa-giudices-prison-diary-details-orange-burgers-fights-201527.

15. "Teresa Giudice—Welcome to Club Fed . . . Enjoy Your Ice Cream!" TMZ, January 5, 2015. Accessed March 12, 2015. www.tmz.com/2015/01/05/teresa-giudice-jail-prison-sentence-money/.

16. Collins and Alvarez, *Prison Ramen*, 26–28.

17. Collins and Alvarez. *Prison Ramen*, 26–28.

18. Collins and Alvarez. *Prison Ramen*, 40–41.

19. Sandra Cate, "'Breaking Bread with a Spread' in a San Francisco County Jail," *Gastronomica* 8, no. 3 (Summer 2008): 17–24. doi: 10.1525/gfc.2008.8.3.17.

20. Cate, "'Breaking Bread with a Spread' in a San Francisco County Jail," 17–24.

21. Doran Larson and B. G. Jacobs, *Fourth City: Essays from the Prison in America* (East Lansing: Michigan State University Press, 2013). 71.

22. Cate, "'Breaking Bread with a Spread' in a San Francisco County Jail," 17–24.

23. Smoyer, "Feeding Relationships," 26–39.

24. Smoyer, "Feeding Relationships," 26–39.

25. Smoyer, "Feeding Relationships," 26–39.

26. "Personal Correspondence," Letter to the author. April 29, 2010.

27. Username: Carmichael106, "Prison Cooking Recipes—Post Them Here!" (Online Discussion Forum.). *PrisonTalk.com*. July 2007. Accessed March 20, 2016. www.prisontalk.com/forums/showthread.php?t=150289&page=18.

28. "Death Letters," *Texas Monthly*, September 2008, 9. Accessed December 10, 2012. ProQuest.

29. Cate, "'Breaking Bread with a Spread' in a San Francisco County Jail," 17–24.

30. Username: Danielle. "Prison Cooking Recipes—Post Them Here!" (Online Discussion Forum.). *PrisonTalk.com*. May 18, 2002. Accessed January 10, 2016. www.prisontalk.com/forums/archive/index.php/t-150289.html.

31. Kevin Bullington, *Creative Snacks, Meals, Beverages and Desserts You Can Make behind Bars: A Cookbook for Inmates (and Others on a Tight Budget) Looking to Put the Fun Back into Food* (Self Published, 2013), 34.

32. Caroline Pardilla, "How to Make Prison Wine (The Craft Version)," *Los Angeles Magazine*, July 1, 2014. Accessed May 21, 2015. www.lamag.com/drinkrecipes/how-to-make-prison-wine-the-craft-version/#sthash.40wfpWXF.dpuf.

33. Patrick Larmour, "Getting a Hustle: How to Live Like a King Behind Bars," *The Marshall Project*, January 1, 2016. www.themarshallproject.org/2016/01/15/getting-a-hustle-how-to-live-like-a-king-behind-bars#.Af5v8vtAg.

## CHAPTER 7

1. Bryan Finoki, "Food for Thinkers: WANTED! Prison Food Writers," *GOOD Magazine*, January 31, 2011. Accessed February 11, 2016. www.good.is/articles/food-for-thinkers-wanted-prison-food-writers.

2. Stephen Kaplan, "The Restorative Benefits of Nature: Toward an Integrative Framework," *Journal of Environmental Psychology* 15, no. 3 (1995): 169–82. doi: 10.1016/0272-4944(95)90001-2.

3. Andrew Flachs, "Food for Thought: The Social Impact of Urban Gardens in the Greater Cleveland Area," *Electronic Green Journal* 1, no. 30 2010): 7. doi: 10.1037/e620412011-038.

4. "Our Hierarchy of Needs," *Psychology Today*, May 23, 2012. Accessed March 7, 2014. www.psychologytoday.com/blog/hide-and-seek/201205/our-hierarchy-needs.

5. Eliza Barclay, "Prison Gardens Help Inmates Grow Their Own Food—And Skills," NPR, January 12, 2014. Accessed March 21, 2016. www.npr.org/sections/thesalt/2014/01/12/261397333/prison-gardens-help-inmates-grow-their-own-food-and-skills.

6. "Research Studies—Insight Garden Program." Insight Garden Program. Accessed November 15, 2015. insightgardenprogram.org/research-studies/.

7. Barclay, "Prison Gardens Help Inmates Grow Their Own Food—And Skills."

8. James Jiler, *Doing Time in the Garden: Life Lessons through Prison Horticulture* (Oakland, CA: New Village Press, 2006).

9. Emily Gilbert, "Five Urban Garden Programs that Are Reaching Inmates and At-Risk Populations," Worldwatch Institute. Accessed November 10, 2015. www.worldwatch.org/five-urban-garden-programs-are-reaching-inmates-and-risk-populations.

10. Rebecca Martinez, "Seven Prison Gardens Stock Local Food Banks," *WUNC*, October 29, 2015. Accessed November 11, 2015. wunc.org/post/seven-prison-gardens-stock-local-food-banks#stream/0.

11. Morgan Bulger, "Six U.S. Correctional Facilities with 'Farm to Prison' Local Food Sourcing Programs," *Seedstock*, January 4, 2015. Accessed January 13, 2015. seedstock.com/2015/01/04/six-u-s-correctional-facilities-with-farm-to-prison-local-food-sourcing-programs/.

12. Lydia O'Connor, "How A Farm-To-Table Program Could Revitalize Prisons," *Huffington Post*, May 28, 2014. Accessed January 13, 2016. www.huffingtonpost.com/2014/05/27/california-inmate-farm-program_n_5400670.html.

13. Thomas Beller, "Angola Prison and the Shadow of Slavery," *The New Yorker*, August 19, 2015. Accessed November 22, 2015. www.newyorker.com/culture/cultural-comment/angola-prison-louisiana-photos.

14. Erik Eckholm, "Bible College Helps Some at Louisiana Prison Find Peace," *New York Times*, October 5, 2013. Accessed November 22, 2015. www.nytimes.com/2013/10/06/us/bible-college-helps-some-at-louisiana-prison-find-peace.html.

15. Aaron Taube, "Here's What It's Like for People Trying to Find a Job after They're Released from Prison." *Business Insider*. October 10, 2014. Accessed November 10, 2015. www.businessinsider.com/getting-a-job-after-prison-2014-10.

16. Lois M. Davis, Robert Bozick, Jennifer L. Steele, Jessica Saunders, and Jeremy N. V. Miles, *Evaluating the Effectiveness of Correctional Education: A Meta-Analysis of Programs That Provide Education to Incarcerated Adults*, Report, 2013. Accessed October 9, 2015. www.rand.org/content/dam/rand/pubs/research_reports/RR200/RR266/RAND_RR266.sum .pdf.

17. Kristin Hunt, "Inside Fife and Drum, the Restaurant Run by Inmates inside a Jail," *Thrillist*, June 9, 2015. Accessed November 10, 2015. www.thrillist.com/eat/nation/prison -food-northeastern-correctional-center-fife-and-drum-restaurant.

18. "Fife and Drum—Northeast Correctional Center, Concord, MA." *Chowhound.* February 11, 2010. Accessed November 21, 2015. www.chowhound.com/post/fife-drum-northeast -correctional-center-concord-ma-687330.

19. Jim Yardley, "Italian Cuisine Worth Going to Prison For." *New York Times*, March 5, 2016. Accessed May 12, 2016. www.nytimes.com/2016/03/06/world/europe/in-milan-diners -go-to-prison-to-get-a-good-meal.html?_r=2.

20. "News and Media," Homeboy Industries. Accessed May 11, 2016. www.homeboyin dustries.org/news-events/.

21. "Women's Prison Gardens: Senior Capstone (Course Description)," Portland State University. Accessed November 20, 2015. capstone.unst.pdx.edu/courses/womens-prison -gardens.

22. Jessica Benko, "The Radical Humaneness of Norway's Halden Prison," *New York Times*, March 26, 2015. Accessed November 22, 2015. www.nytimes.com/2015/03/29/ magazine/the-radical-humaneness-of-norways-halden-prison.html.

23. Christina Sterbenz. "Why Norway's Prison System Is so Successful." *Business Insider.* December 11, 2014. Accessed July 7, 2016. www.businessinsider.com/why-norways -prison-system-is-so-successful-2014-12.

24. Benko, "The Radical Humaneness of Norway's Halden Prison."

25. *Norwegian Prisons*, produced by Joseph Patel and Michael Moynihan, performed by Ryan Duffy, *VICE.* 2011, Accessed November 10, 2015. www.vice.com/video/norwegian -prisons.

26. *Norwegian Prisons.*

27. *Norwegian Prisons.*

28. Benko, "The Radical Humaneness of Norway's Halden Prison."

29. Benko, "The Radical Humaneness of Norway's Halden Prison."

30. Christina Sterbenz and Pamela Engel, "Take a Tour of Norway's Unbelievably Luxurious Prison," *Business Insider.* October 29, 2014. Accessed November 20, 2015. www.business insider.com/tour-of-halden-prison-2014-10.

31. Benko, "The Radical Humaneness of Norway's Halden Prison."

32. Maurice Chammah, "Prison without Punishment," *The Marshall Project*, September 25, 2015. www.themarshallproject.org/2015/09/25/prison-without-punishment#.vAz2hBHXh.

33. Chammah, "Prison Without Punishment."

# CHAPTER 8

1. Carrie Johnson, "For this Released Inmate, Freedom Tastes like Pizza for Breakfast," NPR, November 2, 2015. Accessed December 15, 2015. www.npr.org/2015/11/02/453992907/ for-this-released-inmate-freedom-tastes-like-pizza-for-breakfast.

2. "Prisoners and Prisoner Re-Entry." US Department of Justice. Accessed December 20, 2015. www.justice.gov/archive/fbci/progmenu_reentry.html.

3. "Executions in the United States," Death Penalty Information Center. Accessed June 27, 2015. www.deathpenaltyinfo.org/executions-united-states.

4. "Executions in the United States," Death Penalty Information Center.

5. Denise Lavoie, "Boston Marathon Bomber Arrives at Colorado Prison, Expected to Go to Indiana Death Row," *Toronto Sun*, June 25, 2015. Accessed November 13, 2015. www .torontosun.com/2015/06/25/boston-marathon-bomber-arrives-at-colorado-prison-expected -to-go-to-indiana-death-row.

6. Daniel Lachance, "Last Words, Last Meals, and Last Stands: Agency and Individuality in the Modern Execution Process," *Law and Social Inquiry* 32, no. 3 (2007): 702. doi: 10.1111/j.1747-4469.2007.00074.x.

7. Hannah Goldfield, "Death-Row Dining," *The New Yorker*, September 26, 2014. Accessed December 21, 2015. www.newyorker.com/culture/cultural-comment/death-row-dining.

8. Katherin Baildon, "Food and Brand Lab," A Final Test of Conscience. Accessed January 23, 2016. foodpsychology.cornell.edu/discoveries/final-test-conscience.

9. Lachance, "Last Words, Last Meals, and Last Stands," 714.

10. Christopher Beam, "Can a Prisoner Request Anything for His Last Meal?" *Slate Magazine*, November 10, 2009. Accessed December 22, 2015. www.slate.com/articles/ news_and_politics/explainer/2009/11/ill_have_24_tacos_and_the_filet_mignon.html.

11. Beam, "Can a Prisoner Request Anything for His Last Meal?"

12. Manny Fernandez, "Texas Death Row Kitchen Cooks Its Last 'Last Meal,'" *New York Times*, September 22, 2011. Accessed December 22, 2015. www.nytimes.com/2011/09/23/us/ texas-death-row-kitchen-cooks-its-last-last-meal.html.

13. Daniel Nasaw, "Last Meal: What's the Point of this Death Row Ritual?" BBC News, September 26, 2011. Accessed January 23, 2016. www.bbc.com/news/magazine-15040658.

14. Timothy Williams, "Ex-Inmate Shares Stories of Stint as a Death Row Chef," *New York Times*, October 18, 2011. Accessed December 22, 2015. www.nytimes.com/2011/10/19/ us/former-inmate-shares-tricks-of-the-trade-of-a-death-row-chef.html.

15. Alan White, "12 Pictures of Death Row Prisoners' Last Meals," *BuzzFeed*, February 18, 2014. Accessed December 20, 2015. www.buzzfeed.com/alanwhite/12-pictures-of-death -row-prisoners-last-meals.

16. Brian Wansink, Kevin M. Kniffin, and Mitsuru Shimizu, "Death Row Nutrition: Curious Conclusions of Last Meals," *Appetite* 59, no. 3 (2012): 837–43. doi: 10.1016/j.appet .2012.08.017.

17. Brian Wansink and Kevin M. Kniffin. "Food and Brand Lab." *Death Row Nutrition: Curious Conclusions of Last Meals*. Accessed July 7, 2016. foodpsychology.cornell.edu/ research/death-row-nutrition-curious-conclusions-last-meals.

18. P. Cooey, "Women's Religious Conversions on Death Row: Theorizing Religion and State," *Journal of the American Academy of Religion* 70, no. 4 (2002): 699–718, 700. doi: 10.1093/jaar/70.4.699.

19. Cooey, "Women's Religious Conversions on Death Row," 699–718, 700.

20. "Karla Faye Tucker's Last Hours?" CNN. February 3, 1998. Accessed January 15, 2016. www.cnn.com/US/9802/03/tucker/.

21. Lachance, "Last Words, Last Meals, and Last Stands," 701–24, 714.

22. Carey Goldberg, "Federal Executions Have Been Rare but May Increase," *New York Times*. May 6, 2001. Accessed January 15, 2016. www.nytimes.com/2001/05/06/us/federal -executions-have-been-rare-but-may-increase.html.

23. Henry Hargreaves, "Last Meals of Death Row Inmates," CBS News. Accessed January 15, 2016. www.cbsnews.com/pictures/last-meals-of-death-row/.

24. "Executed Man's Last Request Honored—Pizza for Homeless," CNN, May 10, 2007. Accessed January 15, 2016. www.cnn.com/2007/US/05/09/execution.pizza/.

25. "Movie, Documentary Could Be Adapted from Book by Gacy's Lawyer," CBS Chicago, December 21, 2011. Accessed January 14, 2016. chicago.cbslocal.com/2011/12/21/movie-documentary-could-be-adapted-from-book-by-gacys-lawyer/.

26. Hargreaves, "Last Meals of Death Row Inmates."

27. John Barryman, "The 25 Most Elaborate Final Meals in Death Row History," *Ranker*. Accessed January 15, 2016. www.ranker.com/list/top-10-most-elaborate-final-meals-in-death-row-history/john-barryman?format=SLIDESHOW.

28. Jason DeParle, "Victim's Parents Watch Willie Die," PBS. Accessed March 11, 2015. www.pbs.org/wgbh/pages/frontline/angel/articles/timespicayune1228.html. Reproduction of an article originally run in the *Times-Picayune*.

29. Hargreaves, "Last Meals of Death Row Inmates."

30. Scott McMann, "Last Meal on Death Row: What Would You Order?" *Ghost Theory*, September 23, 2011. Accessed January 20, 2016. www.ghosttheory.com/2011/09/23/last-meal-on-death-row-what-would-you-order.

31. Katie Santich, "Last Man to Die: Who Was Victor Feguer?" *Orlando Sentinel*. June 9, 2001. Accessed January 15, 2016. articles.orlandosentinel.com/2001-06-09/lifestyle/0106080426_1_bartels-victor-wife.

32. Santich, "Last Man To Die: Who Was Victor Feguer?"

33. Hargreaves, "Last Meals of Death Row Inmates."

# Bibliography

"About Us—Trinity Services Group." Trinity Services Group. Accessed March 5, 2015. www.trinityservicesgroup.com/trinity-services-group/.

Adams, John. "Commissary Day." *Pen America*. 2012. Accessed June 11, 2015. www.pen .org/nonfiction/commissary-day.

Alexander, Michelle, and Cornel West. *The New Jim Crow: Mass Incarceration in the Age of Colorblindness*. New York: New Press, 2012.

Alvarez, Lizette. "You Don't Have to Be Jewish to Love a Kosher Prison Meal." *New York Times*. January 20, 2014. Accessed July 15, 2014. www.nytimes.com/2014/01/21/us/you -dont-have-to-be-jewish-to-love-a-kosher-prison-meal.html.

Amurao, Carla. "Fact Sheet: How Bad Is the School-to-Prison Pipeline?" PBS. March 26, 2013. www.pbs.org/wnet/tavissmiley/tsr/education-under-arrest/school-to-prison-pipeline -fact-sheet/.

Anderson, Eric, and Jennifer Peros. "Teresa Giudice Writes about 'Orange' Burgers and Fights in Her Prison Diary." *Us Weekly*. July 2, 2015. Accessed September 12, 2015. www.usmagazine.com/celebrity-news/news/teresa-giudices-prison-diary-details-orange -burgers-fights-201527.

Annas, George J. "Law and the Life Sciences: Prison Hunger Strikes: Why the Motive Matters." *The Hastings Center Report* 12, no. 6 (1982): 21–22.

Associated Press. "AP: Private Prisons Profit from Illegal Immigrants." CBSNews. August 2, 2012. www.cbsnews.com/news/ap-private-prisons-profit-from-illegal-immigrants/.

Associated Press. "Colorado: Ruling on Prison Food." *New York Times* (New York). April 24, 2009. Accessed March 3, 2015. www.nytimes.com/2009/04/25/us/25brfs-RULINGONPRIS _BRF.html.

Associated Press. "Opponents Press Snyder to Cancel Prison Contract." *Toledo Blade.* July 30, 2014. www.toledoblade.com/State/2014/07/30/Opponents-press-Snyder-to-cancel -prison-contract.html.

Baildon, Katherin. "Food and Brand Lab." A Final Test of Conscience. Accessed January 23, 2016. foodpsychology.cornell.edu/discoveries/final-test-conscience.

Barclay, Eliza. "Food as Punishment: Giving U.S. Inmates 'The Loaf' Persists." NPR: *The Salt.* January 2, 2014. Accessed March 17, 2015. www.npr.org/sections/thesalt/ 2014/01/02/256605441/punishing-inmates-with-the-loaf-persists-in-the-u-s.

———. "Prison Gardens Help Inmates Grow Their Own Food—And Skills." NPR. January 12, 2014. Accessed March 21, 2016. www.npr.org/sections/thesalt/2014/01/12/261397333/ prison-gardens-help-inmates-grow-their-own-food-and-skills.

Barnes, Harry Elmer. "Historical Origin of the Prison System in America." *Journal of Criminal Law and Criminology* 12, no. 1 (1921): 35–60.

Barnhardt, Laura. "Loaves Give Rise to Good Behavior." *Baltimore Sun.* March 25, 2002. Accessed May 2, 2014. articles.baltimoresun.com/2002-03-25/news/0203250211_1_ supermax-loaf-lima-bean.

Barryman, John. "The 25 Most Elaborate Final Meals in Death Row History." *Ranker.* Accessed January 15, 2016. www.ranker.com/list/top-10-most-elaborate-final-meals-in -death-row-history/john-barryman?format=SLIDESHOW.

Bassett, Margery. "The Fleet Prison in the Middle Ages." *University of Toronto Law Journal* 5, no. 2 (1944): 383–402.

Beam, Christopher. "Can a Prisoner Request Anything for His Last Meal?" *Slate Magazine.* November 10, 2009. Accessed December 22, 2015. www.slate.com/articles/news_and_ politics/explainer/2009/11/ill_have_24_tacos_and_the_filet_mignon.html.

Beller, Thomas. "Angola Prison and the Shadow of Slavery." *The New Yorker.* August 19, 2015. Accessed November 22, 2015. www.newyorker.com/culture/cultural-comment/angola -prison-louisiana-photos.

Benko, Jessica. "The Radical Humaneness of Norway's Halden Prison." *New York Times.* March 26, 2015. Accessed November 22, 2015. www.nytimes.com/2015/03/29/magazine/ the-radical-humaneness-of-norways-halden-prison.html.

Bosworth, Mary. *Encyclopedia of Prisons and Correctional Facilities.* Thousand Oaks, CA: Sage Publications, 2005.

Boyd, Tim. "Cruel and Unusual Punishment: Soy Diet for Illinois Prisoners—Weston A. Price." Weston A. Price Foundation. May 1, 2009. www.westonaprice.org/health-topics/ cruel-and-unusual-punishment-soy-diet-for-illinois-prisoners/.

Briefel, Ronette R., Mary Kay Crepinsek, Charlotte Cabili, Ander Wilson, and Philip M. Gleason. "School Food Environments and Practices Affect Dietary Behaviors of US Public School Children." *Journal of the American Dietetic Association* 109, no. 2 (2009): Supplement, S91–S107.

Brook, Pete. "Rarely Seen Images of the Real San Quentin." *The Marshall Project.* February 10, 2016. Accessed March 23, 2016. www.themarshallproject.org/2016/02/10/rarely-seen -images-of-the-real-san-quentin.

Bruce, Cara. "Private Prisons: Lowering the Bar to Turn a Buck?" *Young Money.* Accessed March 8, 2016. finance.youngmoney.com/credit_debt/private-prisons-lowering-the-bar-to -turn-a-buck/.

Brunon-Ernst, Anne. *Beyond Foucault: New Perspectives on Bentham's Panopticon.* Farnham, UK: Ashgate, 2012.

Bulger, Morgan. "Six U.S. Correctional Facilities With 'Farm to Prison' Local Food Sourcing Programs." *Seedstock.* January 4, 2015. Accessed January 13, 2015. seedstock.com/2015/01/ 04/six-u-s-correctional-facilities-with-farm-to-prison-local-food-sourcing-programs/.

Bullington, Kevin. *Creative Snacks, Meals, Beverages and Desserts You Can Make behind Bars: A Cookbook for Inmates (and Others on a Tight Budget) Looking to Put the Fun Back into Food.* Self-published, 2013.

*Bureau of Justice Statistics: Prisoners in 2014.* Report no. NCJ 248955. www.bjs.gov/content/pub/pdf/p14_Summary.pdf.

Carpenter, Kenneth J. "Nutritional Studies in Victorian Prisons." *Journal of Nutrition* 136, no. 1 (January 2006): 1–8.

Carroll, Rory. "California Inmates Launch Biggest Hunger Strike in State's History." *Guardian.* 2013. Accessed March 17, 2015. www.theguardian.com/world/2013/jul/09/california-prisoners-hunger-strike.

Cate, Sandra. "'Breaking Bread with a Spread' in a San Francisco County Jail." *Gastronomica* 8, no. 3 (Summer 2008): 17–24. doi:10.1525/gfc.2008.8.3.17.

Center for Constitutional Rights. "Summary of Settlement Terms in Anti-solitary Confinement Class Action, *Ashker v. Brown.*" *San Francisco Bay View.* September 26, 2015. Accessed April 17, 2015. sfbayview.com/2015/09/summary-of-settlement-terms-in-anti-solitary-confinement-class-action-ashker-v-brown/.

Chammah, Maurice. "Prison without Punishment." *The Marshall Project.* September 25, 2015. www.themarshallproject.org/2015/09/25/prison-without-punishment#.vAz2hBHXh.

Chang, Tracy F. H., and Douglas E. Thompkins. "Corporations Go to Prisons: The Expansion of Corporate Power in the Correctional Industry." *Labor Studies Journal* 27, no. 1 (2002): 45–69. Project Muse.

Chediac, Joyce. "Punishment for Profit: The Economics of Mass Incarceration." *Workers World.* 2015. www.workers.org/articles/2015/05/04/punishment-for-profit-the-economics-of-mass-incarceration/.

"Chilies Aid Sumatra Jail Break." BBC News. August 22, 2006. Accessed May 2, 2015. news.bbc.co.uk/2/hi/asia-pacific/5274924.stm.

Coates, Ta-Nehisi. "The Black Family in the Age of Mass Incarceration." *Atlantic.* October 2015. www.theatlantic.com/magazine/archive/2015/10/the-black-family-in-the-age-of-mass-incarceration/403246/.

Cohen, Adam. "Can Food Be Cruel and Unusual Punishment?" *TIME.com.* April 2, 2012. Accessed March 17, 2015. ideas.time.com/2012/04/02/can-food-be-cruel-and-unusual-punishment/.

Cohn, S. K. "The Medieval Prison: A Social History." *English Historical Review* CXXV, no. 512 (2010): 153–55.

Collins, Clifton, and Gustavo Alvarez. *Prison Ramen: Recipes and Stories from behind Bars.* New York: Workman, 2015.

Cooey, P. "Women's Religious Conversions on Death Row: Theorizing Religion and State." *Journal of the American Academy of Religion* 70, no. 4 (2002): 699–718. doi: 10.1093/jaar/70.4.699.

"Correctional Facilities Food Services." Aramark. Accessed December 1, 2015. www.aramark.com/industries/business-government/correctional-facilities/food-services.

Cross, Maria, and Barbara MacDonald. *Nutrition in Institutions.* Chichester, West Sussex: Wiley-Blackwell, 2009.

"Cruel and Unusual Punishment." *The Legal Dictionary / The Free Dictionary.* Accessed March 3, 2015. legal-dictionary.thefreedictionary.com/Cruel and Unusual Punishment.

Curry, Colleen. "Michigan Is Booting Aramark from Its Prisons, but Not Over Rat-and-Maggot-Tainted Food." *VICE News.* July 14, 2015. news.vice.com/article/michigan-is-booting-aramark-from-its-prisons-but-not-over-rat-and-maggot-tainted-food.

"Daily Cost to Feed Prisoners and the Average American." Prison Policy Initiative. Accessed May 24, 2015. www.prisonpolicy.org/graphs/foodcosts.html.

Davidson, Jacob. "'America's Toughest Sheriff' Takes Meat off Jail Menu." *TIME*. September 27, 2013. newsfeed.time.com/2013/09/27/americas-toughest-sheriff-takes-meat-off-jail-menu/.

Davis, Lois. "To Stop Prisons' Revolving Door." *Los Angeles Times*. September 16, 2013. Accessed June 1, 2014. articles.latimes.com/2013/sep/16/opinion/la-oe-davis-prison-education-20130916.

Davis, Lois M., Robert Bozick, Jennifer L. Steele, Jessica Saunders, and Jeremy N. V. Miles. *Evaluating the Effectiveness of Correctional Education: A Meta-Analysis of Programs That Provide Education to Incarcerated Adults*. Report. 2013. Accessed October 9, 2015. www.rand.org/content/dam/rand/pubs/research_reports/RR200/RR266/RAND_RR266.sum.pdf.

"Death Letters." *Texas Monthly*. September 2008: 9. Accessed December 10, 2012. ProQuest.

DeParle, Jason. "Victim's Parents Watch Willie Die." PBS. Accessed March 11, 2015. www.pbs.org/wgbh/pages/frontline/angel/articles/timespicayune1228.html. Reproduction of an article originally run in the *Times-Picayune*.

DeVille, Milo. "Literature on Lockdown: Chow in Prison." *Missouri Review*. August 1, 2014. Accessed April 17, 2015. www.missourireview.com/tmr-blog/2014/08/literature-on-lockdown-chow-in-prison/.

"Did Lil Wayne Order Kool-Aid in Jail? Oh Yeah!" TMZ. August 16, 2010. Accessed October 2, 2014. www.tmz.com/2010/08/15/lil-wayne-jail-kool-aid-rikers-island-food.

"THE DME.COM LIST OF THE TOP TEN LAST MEALS." Dead Man Eating. December 13, 2003. Accessed May 9, 2014. deadmaneating.blogspot.com/2003_12_07_archive.html.

*The Drug War, Mass Incarceration and Race*. Report. 2015. www.drugpolicy.org/resource/drug-war-mass-incarceration-and-race.

Eckholm, Erik. "Bible College Helps Some at Louisiana Prison Find Peace." *New York Times*. October 5, 2013. Accessed November 22, 2015. www.nytimes.com/2013/10/06/us/bible-college-helps-some-at-louisiana-prison-find-peace.html.

Egan, Paul. "Aramark Prison Worker Suspected in Attempted Hired Hit." *Detroit Free Press*. September 25, 2014. Accessed March 8, 2016. www.freep.com/story/news/local/michigan/2014/09/25/aramark-worker-investigated-murder-hire-plot/16172713/.

———. "Maggots Prompt Call for Prison Kitchen Inspections." *Detroit Free Press*. Accessed June 24, 2015. www.freep.com/story/news/local/michigan/2015/06/24/bill-targets-aramark-requiring-prison-kitchen-inspections/29210815/.

"Eighth Amendment." *The Free Dictionary—Legal Dictionary*. Accessed February 12, 2014. legal-dictionary.thefreedictionary.com/Eighth Amendment.

Elliot, Justin. "What Is Nutraloaf, Anyway?" *Mother Jones*. July 2008. Accessed March 17, 2015. www.motherjones.com/politics/2008/07/what-nutraloaf-anyway.

Engber, Daniel. "What Martha Really Ate in Prison." *Slate*. March 3, 2005. Accessed December 11, 2012. www.slate.com/articles/news_and_politics/explainer/2005/03/what_martha_really_ate_in_prison.html.

"Executed Man's Last Request Honored—Pizza for Homeless." CNN. May 10, 2007. Accessed January 15, 2016. www.cnn.com/2007/US/05/09/execution.pizza/.

"Executions in the United States." Death Penalty Information Center. Accessed June 27, 2015. www.deathpenaltyinfo.org/executions-united-states.

Farber, Bernard J., ed. "Prisoner Diet Legal Issues." *AELE Monthly Law Journal* 2007, no. 7 (July 2007). www.aele.org/law/2007JBJUL/2007-07MLJ301.pdf.

Federal Bureau of Prisons. Department of Justice. *Bureau of Prisons*. April 22, 1996. Accessed October 4, 2014. www.bop.gov/policy/progstat/4761_004.pdf. Program Statement: 4761.04.

———. *Food Service Manual*. September 13, 2011. Accessed October 10, 2015. www.bop.gov/policy/progstat/4700_006.pdf. Number: P4700.06.

————. *Management of Diabetes—Federal Bureau of Prisons Clinical Practice Guidelines.* June 2012. Accessed October 10, 2015. www.bop.gov/resources/pdfs/diabetes.pdf.

Feldscher, Kyle. "After Aramark Issues, Lawmakers Propose Having Local Health Departments Inspect Prison Kitchens." *Michigan Live.* June 25, 2015. www.mlive.com/lansing -news/index.ssf/2015/06/after_aramark_issues_lawmakers.html.

Fernandez, Manny. "Texas Death Row Kitchen Cooks Its Last 'Last Meal.'" *New York Times.* September 22, 2011. Accessed December 22, 2015. www.nytimes.com/2011/09/23/us/ texas-death-row-kitchen-cooks-its-last-last-meal.html.

"Fife and Drum—Northeast Correctional Center, Concord, MA." *Chowhound.* February 11, 2010. Accessed November 21, 2015. www.chowhound.com/post/fife-drum-northeast -correctional-center-concord-ma-687330.

Finoki, Bryan. "Food for Thinkers: WANTED! Prison Food Writers." *GOOD Magazine.* January 31, 2011. Accessed February 11, 2016. www.good.is/articles/food-for-thinkers -wanted-prison-food-writers.

Fishbein, Diana, and Susan Pease. "The Effects of Diet on Behavior: Implications for Criminology and Corrections." *Research in Corrections* 1, no. 2 (June 1988). Accessed July 7, 2016. static.nicic.gov/Library/006777.pdf.

Fishman, Steve. "Bernie Madoff, Free at Last." *NYMag.com.* June 6, 2010. Accessed June 1, 2015. nymag.com/news/crimelaw/66468/index3.html.

Flachs, Andrew. "Food for Thought: The Social Impact of Urban Gardens in the Greater Cleveland Area." *Electronic Green Journal* 1, no. 30 (2010): 7. doi: 10.1037/e620412011 -038.

"Food to Blame for Northpoint Prison Riot?" ABC36TV. November 6, 2009. Accessed March 11, 2015. www.youtube.com/watch?v=ruo80t0c-24.

Foucault, Michel. *Discipline and Punish: The Birth of the Prison.* New York: Vintage Books, 1995.

Fresh Air. "How 4 Inmates Launched A Statewide Hunger Strike From Solitary." Advertisement. NPR. March 6, 2014. Accessed March 17, 2015. www.npr.org/templates/transcript/ transcript.php?storyId=286794055.

Gesch, C. B. "Influence of Supplementary Vitamins, Minerals and Essential Fatty Acids on the Antisocial Behaviour of Young Adult Prisoners: Randomised, Placebo-controlled Trial." *British Journal of Psychiatry* 181, no. 1 (2002): 22–28.

Giang, Vivian. "Inmate Talks to Us Over an Illegal Cell Phone about Working the Jailhouse Black Market." *Business Insider.* July 2, 2012. www.businessinsider.com/prisoner-shares -with-us-a-glimpse-of-the-hustle-behind-bars-2012-6.

Gilbert, Emily. "Five Urban Garden Programs that Are Reaching Inmates and At-Risk Populations." Worldwatch Institute. Accessed November 10, 2015. www.worldwatch.org/five -urban-garden-programs-are-reaching-inmates-and-risk-populations.

Glaze, Lauren, and Danielle Kaeble. *Correctional Populations in the United States, 2013.* Report no. NCJ 248479. December 2014. www.bjs.gov/content/pub/pdf/cpus13.pdf.

Godderis, Rebecca. "Food for Thought: An Analysis of Power and Identity in Prison Food Narratives." *Berkeley Journal of Sociology* 50 (2006): 61–75. www.jstor.org/stable/41035612.

Goldberg, Carey. "Federal Executions Have Been Rare but May Increase." *New York Times.* May 6, 2001. Accessed January 15, 2016. www.nytimes.com/2001/05/06/us/federal -executions-have-been-rare-but-may-increase.html.

Goldfield, Hannah. "Death-Row Dining." *The New Yorker.* September 26, 2014. Accessed December 21, 2015. www.newyorker.com/culture/cultural-comment/death-row-dining.

Gopnik, Adam. "The Caging of America: Why Do We Lock Up so Many People?" *The New Yorker.* January 30, 2012. www.newyorker.com/magazine/2012/01/30/the-caging-of -america.

Griffiths, Arthur. *Memorials of Millbank, and Chapters in Prison History*. London: Chapman and Hall, 1884.

Gusmaroli, Danielle. "LI-LO LIVES ON JELLY FOR 14 DAYS IN JAIL; Freed Lohan Heads Straight into Rehab Unit." *Daily Record* (Glasgow, Scotland). August 3, 2010. Accessed December 3, 2012. www.highbeam.com/doc/1G1-233367758.html?refid=easy _hf.

Hardy, Kathy. "Nutrition Services in Correctional Facilities." *Today's Dietitian*. June 2016. Accessed July 07, 2016. www.todaysdietitian.com/newarchives/0616p32.shtml.

Hargreaves, Henry. "Last Meals of Death Row Inmates." CBSNews. Accessed January 15, 2016. www.cbsnews.com/pictures/last-meals-of-death-row/.

Henrichson, Christian, and Ruth Delaney. *The Price of Prisons: What Incarceration Costs Taxpayers*. Report. July 20, 2012. www.vera.org/sites/default/files/resources/downloads/ price-of-prisons-updated-version-021914.pdf.

"Highest to Lowest—Prison Population Total." *World Prison Brief*. Accessed May 14, 2015. www.prisonstudies.org/highest-to-lowest/prison-population-total.

Howard, John. *The State of the Prisons in England and Wales*. Cambridge, UK: Cambridge University Press, 2013.

Hunt, Kristin. "Inside Fife and Drum, the Restaurant Run by Inmates Inside a Jail." *Thrillist*. June 9, 2015. Accessed November 10, 2015. www.thrillist.com/eat/nation/prison-food -northeastern-correctional-center-fife-and-drum-restaurant.

"Incarceration." The Sentencing Project. Accessed February 10, 2015. www.sentencingproject .org/issues/incarceration/.

James, Scott. "Jail Time Yields a Clash on Vegetarian Meals." *New York Times*. August 4, 2011. Accessed December 28, 2014. www.nytimes.com/2011/08/05/us/05bcjames.html.

Jiler, James. *Doing Time in the Garden: Life Lessons through Prison Horticulture*. Oakland, CA: New Village Press, 2006.

"John Howard (1726–1790)." BBC. Accessed June 12, 2015. www.bbc.co.uk/history/ historic_figures/howard_john.shtml.

Johnson, Carrie. "For this Released Inmate, Freedom Tastes like Pizza for Breakfast." NPR. November 2, 2015. Accessed December 15, 2015. www.npr.org/2015/11/02/453992907/ for-this-released-inmate-freedom-tastes-like-pizza-for-breakfast.

Judd, Alan. "Jail Food Complaints Highlight Debate over Outsourcing Public Services." *Atlanta Journal-Constitution*. January 1, 2015. www.myajc.com/news/news/public-affairs/ jail-food-complaints-highlight-debate-over-outsour/njZh3/.

Kaeble, Danielle, Lauren Glaze, Anastasios Tsoutis, and Todd Minton. *Bureau of Justice Statistics: Correctional Populations in the United States, 2014*. Report no. NCJ 249513. January 21, 2016. www.bjs.gov/content/pub/pdf/cpus14.pdf.

Kafka, Franz, and Joachim Neugroschel. *The Metamorphosis, In the Penal Colony, and Other Stories: With Two New Stories*. New York: Scribner Paperback Fiction, 2000.

Kaplan, Stephen. "The Restorative Benefits of Nature: Toward an Integrative Framework." *Journal of Environmental Psychology* 15, no. 3 (1995): 169–82. doi:10.1016/0272 -4944(95)90001-2.

Katz, Stephen. "What It's Like to Eat Some of the Worst Prison Food in America." *VICE News*. September 25, 2015. munchies.vice.com/en/articles/what-its-like-to-eat-some-of -the-worst-prison-food-in-america.

Kniffin, Kevin, and Brian Wansink. "Death Row Confessions and the Last Meal Test of Innocence." *Laws* 3, no. 1 (2013): 1–11. doi: 10.3390/laws3010001.

Kohut, Margaret R. *When You Have to Go to Prison: A Complete Guide for You and Your Family*. Ocala, FL: Atlantic Publishing Group, 2011.

Lach, Eric. "Joe Arpaio Brags about Serving Inmates 56 Cent Thanksgiving Dinner." *Talking Points Memo*. November 29, 2013. Accessed May 2, 2014. talkingpointsmemo.com/livewire/joe-arpaio-brags-about-serving-inmates-56-cent-thanksgiving-dinner.

Lachance, Daniel. "Last Words, Last Meals, and Last Stands: Agency and Individuality in the Modern Execution Process." *Law and Social Inquiry* 32, no. 3 (2007): 701–24. doi: 10.1111/j.1747-4469.2007.00074.x.

Larmour, Patrick. "Getting a Hustle: How to Live Like a King Behind Bars." *The Marshall Project*. January 1, 2016. www.themarshallproject.org/2016/01/15/getting-a-hustle-how-to-live-like-a-king-behind-bars#.Af5v8vtAg.

Larson, Doran, and B. G. Jacobs. *Fourth City: Essays from the Prison in America*. East Lansing: Michigan State University Press, 2013.

Lavoie, Denise. "Boston Marathon Bomber Arrives at Colorado Prison, Expected to Go to Indiana Death Row." *Toronto Sun*. June 25, 2015. Accessed November 13, 2015. www.torontosun.com/2015/06/25/boston-marathon-bomber-arrives-at-colorado-prison-expected-to-go-to-indiana-death-row.

Lawrence, Felicity. "Omega-3, Junk Food and the Link between Violence and What We Eat." *Guardian*. October 17, 2006. Accessed May 12, 2015. www.theguardian.com/politics/2006/oct/17/prisonsandprobation.ukcrime.

Maraglino, Dorothy. "Dorothy Maraglino on Prison: Part 1—Prison Writers." *Prison Writers*. Accessed June 21, 2015. www.prisonwriters.com/dorothy-maraglino-on-prison-part-one/.

Marquart, J. W., and J. B. Roebuck. "Institutional Control and the Christmas Festival in a Maximum Security Penitentiary." *Journal of Contemporary Ethnography* 15, no. 3–4 (October 1987): 449–73. doi: 10.1177/089124168701500307.

Martinez, Rebecca. "Seven Prison Gardens Stock Local Food Banks." *WUNC*. October 29, 2015. Accessed November 11, 2015. wunc.org/post/seven-prison-gardens-stock-local-food-banks#stream/0.

McCaffrey, Shannon. "Prison Blues: States Slimming Down Inmate Meals." *November Coalition*. June 5, 2009. www.november.org/stayinfo/breaking09/Prison_Blues_Inmate_Meals.html.

Mckinley, Jesse. "New York Prisons Take an Unsavory Punishment off the Table." *New York Times*. December 17, 2015. Accessed April 12, 2015. www.nytimes.com/2015/12/18/nyregion/new-york-prisons-take-an-unsavory-punishment-off-the-table.html?_r=0.

McMann, Scott. "Last Meal on Death Row: What Would You Order?" *Ghost Theory*. September 23, 2011. Accessed January 20, 2016. www.ghosttheory.com/2011/09/23/last-meal-on-death-row-what-would-you-order.

"Miss Alice Paul on Hunger Strike." *New York Times*. November 7, 1917. Accessed April 10, 2015. query.nytimes.com/mem/archive-free/pdf?res=9A04E7D9123FE433A25754C0A9679D946696D6CF.

"Movie, Documentary Could Be Adapted from Book by Gacy's Lawyer." CBS Chicago. December 21, 2011. Accessed January 14, 2016. chicago.cbslocal.com/2011/12/21/movie-documentary-could-be-adapted-from-book-by-gacys-lawyer/.

Myers, Dan. "What Did the World's Most Notorious Criminals Request for Their Last Meals?" Fox News. February 26, 2015. Accessed January 5, 2016. www.foxnews.com/leisure/2015/02/26/what-did-world-most-notorious-criminals-request-for-their-last-meals/.

Naim, Cyrus. "Prison Food Law." Master's thesis, Harvard University, 2005. Accessed March 2, 2015. nrs.harvard.edu/urn-3:HUL.InstRepos:8848245.

Nasaw, Daniel. "Last Meal: What's the Point of this Death Row Ritual?" BBC News. September 26, 2011. Accessed January 23, 2016. www.bbc.com/news/magazine-15040658.

Negri, Antonio. *The Savage Anomaly: The Power of Spinoza's Metaphysics and Politics*. Minneapolis: University of Minnesota Press, 1991.

Nestle, Marion. "Good News: Obesity Rates Leveling Off. But How Come?" *Food Politics*. January 22, 2012. www.foodpolitics.com/2012/01/good-news-obesity-rates-leveling-off -how-come/.

———. *Food Politics: How the Food Industry Influences Nutrition and Health*. Berkeley: University of California Press, 2007.

"News and Media." Homeboy Industries. Accessed May 11, 2016. www.homeboyindustries .org/news-events/.

*New York Times* (New York). "America's Worst Sheriff (Joe Arpaio)." Editorial. December 31, 2008. theboard.blogs.nytimes.com/2008/12/31/americas-worst-sheriff-joe-arpaio/?_r=0.

*Norwegian Prisons*. Produced by Joseph Patel and Michael Moynihan. Performed by Ryan Duffy. *VICE*. 2011. Accessed November 10, 2015. www.vice.com/video/norwegian -prisons.

O'Connor, Lydia. "How A Farm-To-Table Program Could Revitalize Prisons." *Huffington Post*. May 28, 2014. Accessed January 13, 2016. www.huffingtonpost.com/2014/05/27/ california-inmate-farm-program_n_5400670.html.

"Office of the Inspector General—A Message from Inspector General Robert A. Barton." Homepage. Accessed October 1, 2015. www.oig.ca.gov/.

Olson, Samantha. "I Ate Like a Prisoner for a Week—Here's What Happened." *Medical Daily*. April 27, 2015. Accessed October 11, 2015. www.medicaldaily.com/1-week-prison -food-diet-reveals-problems-inmate-meals-low-cost-bad-taste-and-very-349572.

Orson, Diane. "'Million-Dollar Blocks' Map Incarceration's Costs." NPR. October 2, 2012. www.npr.org/2012/10/02/162149431/million-dollar-blocks-map-incarcerations-costs.

"Our Hierarchy of Needs." *Psychology Today*. May 23, 2012. Accessed March 7, 2014. www .psychologytoday.com/blog/hide-and-seek/201205/our-hierarchy-needs.

Pardilla, Caroline. "How to Make Prison Wine (The Craft Version)." *Los Angeles Magazine*. July 1, 2014. Accessed May 21, 2015. www.lamag.com/drinkrecipes/how-to-make-prison -wine-the-craft-version/#sthash.40wfpWXF.dpuf.

"Personal Correspondence." Letter to the author. April 29, 2010.

Piña, Pablo. "Pelican Bay (SHU) Photograph, Canteen List and Menu." *Between the Bars*. December 1, 2013. betweenthebars.org/posts/14975/pelican-bayshu-photograph-canteen -list-and-menu.

Priestley, Philip. *Victorian Prison Lives: English Prison Biography, 1830–1914*. London: Methuen, 1985.

"The Prison Crisis." American Civil Liberties Union. Accessed May 20, 2015. www.aclu .org/prison-crisis.

"Prisoners and Prisoner Re-Entry." US Department of Justice. Accessed December 20, 2015. www.justice.gov/archive/fbci/progmenu_reentry.html.

Pugh, R. B. *Imprisonment in Medieval England*. London: Cambridge University Press, 1968.

"Quality and Nutritional Assurance." Trinity Services Group. Accessed March 5, 2015. www .trinityservicesgroup.com/quality-nutritional-assurance/.

"Racial Disparities in Criminal Justice." American Civil Liberties Union. Accessed July 13, 2015. www.aclu.org/issues/mass-incarceration/racial-disparities-criminal-justice.

"Recidivism." National Institute of Justice. Accessed May 20, 2015. www.nij.gov/topics/ corrections/recidivism/pages/welcome.aspx.

*Recipe for Nutriloaf*. 2012. *Milwaukee Wisconsin Journal Sentenial*, Milwaukee. media.jsonline .com/images/JAILFOOD15G.jpg.

Rein, Lisa. "After Firestorm, Pork Roast Is Back on the Menu at Federal Prisons." *Washington Post*. October 16, 2015. www.washingtonpost.com/news/federal-eye/wp/2015/10/16/ after-firestorm-pork-roast-is-back-on-the-menu-at-federal-prisons/.

———. "Finally, the Government Has Decided to Eliminate Pork—From the Menu in Federal Prisons." *Washington Post*. October 9, 2015. www.washingtonpost.com/news/federal-eye/wp/2015/10/09/finally-the-government-has-decided-to-eliminate-pork-from-the-menu-in-federal-prisons/.

Reiter Anna. "Alice Paul and Her Fight for Women's Suffrage." *Armstrong Undergraduate Journal of History*. Accessed June 10, 2015. archive.armstrong.edu/Initiatives/history_journal/history_journal_fearless_radicalism_alice_paul_and_her_fight_for_womens_suf.

"Religious Land Use and Institutionalized Persons Act." US Department of Justice. August 6, 2015. Accessed April 17, 2016. www.justice.gov/crt/religious-land-use-and-institutionalized-persons-act.

"Research Studies—Insight Garden Program." Insight Garden Program. Accessed November 15, 2015. insightgardenprogram.org/research-studies/.

Restrepo, Claudia. "Is this Prison Food Cruel and Unusual?" *Buzzfeed*. January 12, 2015. Accessed April 12, 2015. www.buzzfeed.com/claudiarestrepo/adults-try-prison-food.

Reutter, David. "Appalling Prison and Jail Food Leaves Prisoners Hungry for Justice." *Prison Legal News*. April 5, 2010. www.prisonlegalnews.org/news/2010/apr/15/appalling-prison-and-jail-food-leaves-prisoners-hungry-for-justice/.

Reutter, David M. "Food Problems Contribute to Riot at Kentucky Prison." *Prison Legal News*. April 15, 2010. Accessed May 7, 2015. www.prisonlegalnews.org/news/2010/apr/15/food-problems-contribute-to-riot-at-kentucky-prison/.

Ridgeway, James, and Jean Cassella. "America's 10 Worst Prisons: Pelican Bay." *Mother Jones*. May 8, 2013. Accessed April 17, 2015. www.motherjones.com/politics/2013/05/10-worst-prisons-america-pelican-bay.

Roberts, Dorothy E. "The Social and Moral Cost of Mass Incarceration in African American Communities." *Stanford Law Review* 56, no. 5 (April 2004): 1275–1305. www.jstor.org/stable/40040178.

Ross, Alice. "Health and Diet in 19th-century America: A Food Historian's Point of View." *Historical Archaeology* 27, no. 2 (1993): 42–56.

Ruby, Jeff. "Dining Critic Tries Nutraloaf, the Prison Food for Misbehaving Inmates." *Chicago Magazine*. August 26, 2010. Accessed March 17, 2015. www.chicagomag.com/Chicago-Magazine/September-2010/Dining-Critic-Tries-Nutraloaf-the-Prison-Food-for-Misbehaving-Inmates/.

Santich, Katie. "Last Man to Die: Who Was Victor Feguer?" *Orlando Sentinel*. June 9, 2001. Accessed January 15, 2016. articles.orlandosentinel.com/2001-06-09/lifestyle/0106080426_1_bartels-victor-wife.

Santora, Marc. "City's Annual Cost per Inmate Is $168,000, Study Finds." *New York Times*. 2013. www.nytimes.com/2013/08/24/nyregion/citys-annual-cost-per-inmate-is-nearly-168000-study-says.html.

Schlosser, Eric. "The Prison-Industrial Complex." *The Atlantic*. December 1998.

"School Meal Trends and Stats." SchoolNutrition.org. Accessed June 11, 2015. schoolnutrition.org/AboutSchoolMeals/SchoolMealTrendsStats/.

"Seeking Accreditation." American Correctional Association. www.aca.org/ACA_Prod_IMIS/ACA_Member/Standards___Accreditation/Seeking_Accreditation/ACA_Member/Standards_and_Accreditation/Seeking_Accreditation_Home.aspx.

Siporin, Steve. "The Kosher Con Game: Who's Keeping Kosher in Prison?" *Western Folklore* 74, no. 1 (Winter 2015): 58–79.

Smoyer, Amy B. "Feeding Relationships: Foodways and Social Networks in a Women's Prison." *Affilia* 30, no. 1 (2014): 26–39. doi: 10.1177/0886109914537490.

Starr, Sonja B., and M. Marit Rehavi. "Mandatory Sentencing and Racial Disparity: Assessing the Role of Prosecutors and the Effects of Booker." *Yale Law Journal*, 2nd ser., 123, no. 1 (October 2013). Accessed July 2, 2015. www.yalelawjournal.org/article/mandatory-sentencing-and-racial-disparity-assessing-the-role-of-prosecutors-and-the-effects-of-booker.

Sterbenz, Christina. "The Modern Prison System Was Created in Benjamin Franklin's Living Room." *Business Insider*. April 19, 2015. www.businessinsider.com/the-worlds-first-prison-was-created-in-benjamin-franklins-living-room-2015-3.

———. "Why Norway's Prison System Is so Successful." *Business Insider*. December 11, 2014. Accessed July 07, 2016. www.businessinsider.com/why-norways-prison-system-is-so-successful-2014-12.

Sterbenz, Christina, and Pamela Engel. "Take a Tour of Norway's Unbelievably Luxurious Prison." *Business Insider*. October 29, 2014. Accessed November 20, 2015. www.businessinsider.com/tour-of-halden-prison-2014-10.

*Tampa Bay Times* (Tampa Bay). "Food Fiasco Costs Inmates, Taxpayers." Editorial. May 14, 2008.

"A Taste of Lobster History." History.com. Accessed October 11, 2015. www.history.com/news/a-taste-of-lobster-history.

Taube, Aaron. "Here's What It's Like for People Trying to Find a Job after They're Released from Prison." *Business Insider*. October 10, 2014. Accessed November 10, 2015. www.businessinsider.com/getting-a-job-after-prison-2014-10.

"Teresa Giudice—Welcome to Club Fed . . . Enjoy Your Ice Cream!" TMZ. January 5, 2015. Accessed March 12, 2015. www.tmz.com/2015/01/05/teresa-giudice-jail-prison-sentence-money/.

Thompson, Christie. "When Your Insulin Pump Is Contraband." *The Marshall Project*. April 22, 2015. Accessed December 12, 2015. www.themarshallproject.org/2015/04/22/when-your-insulin-pump-is-contraband.

"Top 10 Vegetarian-Friendly Prisons!" PETA Top 10 Vegetarian-Friendly Prisons Comments. December 10, 2007. Accessed November 23, 2014. www.peta.org/blog/top-10-vegetarian friendly-prisons/.

Townsend, Elisabeth. *Lobster: A Global History*. London: Reaktion Books, 2011.

Ugelvik, T. "The Hidden Food: Mealtime Resistance and Identity Work in a Norwegian Prison." *Punishment and Society* 13, no. 1 (2011): 47–63.

*US Department of Justice Federal Bureau of Prisons Food Service Manual*. Report no. P4700.06. September 13, 2011. www.bop.gov/policy/progstat/4700_006.pdf.

Username: Carmichael106. "Prison Cooking Recipes—Post Them Here!" (Online Discussion Forum.). *PrisonTalk.com*. July 2007. Accessed March 20, 2016. www.prisontalk.com/forums/showthread.php?t=150289&page=18.

Username: Danielle. "Prison Cooking Recipes—Post Them Here!" (Online Discussion Forum.). *PrisonTalk.com*. May 18, 2002. Accessed January 10, 2016. www.prisontalk.com/forums/archive/index.php/t-150289.html.

"U.S. Prison Population Declined for Third Consecutive Year during 2012." News release, July 25, 2013. Bureau of Justice Statistics. http://www.bjs.gov/content/pub/press/p12acpr.cfm.

Valdez, Tito David, Jr. "Prison Chow Time—If It's Prison Food, It All Tastes the Same." *Inmate.com*. Accessed May 17, 2015. www.inmate.com/prison-articles/prison-chow-time.htm.

Waite, Jennifer. "Prison Food: What Are America's Inmates Eating?" *Inmate Aid*. April 9, 2009. www.inmateaid.com/pages/details/prison-food-what-are-americas-inmates-eating-yahoo.

Wallace-Wells, Benjamin. "The Plot from Solitary." *New York Magazine*. February 26, 2014. Accessed March 17, 2015. nymag.com/news/features/solitary-secure-housing-units-2014-2/.

Wansink, Brian, and Kevin M. Kniffin. "Food and Brand Lab." *Death Row Nutrition: Curious Conclusions of Last Meals*. Accessed July 7, 2016. foodpsychology.cornell.edu/research/death-row-nutrition-curious-conclusions-last-meals.

Wansink, Brian, Kevin M. Kniffin, and Mitsuru Shimizu. "Death Row Nutrition: Curious Conclusions of Last Meals." *Appetite* 59, no. 3 (2012): 837–43. doi: 10.1016/j.appet.2012.08.017.

Ward, Judith. *Ambushed*. London: Vermilion, 1993.

Warren, Jennifer. "For 14 Years, Inmates Have Been Fed for $2.45 a Day." *Los Angeles Times*. June 17, 2002. articles.latimes.com/2002/jun/17/local/me-confood17.

Wartman, Kristin. "Why Food Belongs in Our Discussions of Race." *Civil Eats*. September 3, 2015. civileats.com/2015/09/03/why-food-belongs-in-our-discussions-of-race/.

Weichselbaum, Simone. "This Is Rikers ('They Let You Kiss Twice')." *The Marshall Project*. June 28, 2015. www.themarshallproject.org/2015/06/28/this-is-rikers#.sUxQQvS8N.

"What Foods Do Inmates Eat in Prison?" *Quora*. Accessed March 2, 2015. www.quora.com/What-foods-do-inmates-eat-in-prison.

White, Alan. "12 Pictures of Death Row Prisoners' Last Meals." *BuzzFeed*. February 18, 2014. Accessed December 20, 2015. www.buzzfeed.com/alanwhite/12-pictures-of-death-row-prisoners-last-meals.

Wilde, Oscar. *The Ballad of Reading Gaol*. New York: E. P. Dutton, 1928.

Williams, Timothy. "Ex-Inmate Shares Stories of Stint as a Death Row Chef." *New York Times*. October 18, 2011. Accessed December 22, 2015. www.nytimes.com/2011/10/19/us/former-inmate-shares-tricks-of-the-trade-of-a-death-row-chef.html.

Wilson, Donovan W. "Prison Food: Not Fancy, But—." *New York Times*. 1982. www.nytimes.com/1982/12/19/nyregion/prison-food-not-fancy-but.html.

"Women's Prison Gardens: Senior Capstone (Course Description)." Portland State University. Accessed November 20, 2015. capstone.unst.pdx.edu/courses/womens-prison-gardens.

Yardley, Jim. "Italian Cuisine Worth Going to Prison For." *New York Times*. March 5, 2016. Accessed May 12, 2016. www.nytimes.com/2016/03/06/world/europe/in-milan-diners-go-to-prison-to-get-a-good-meal.html?_r=2.

Ye Hee Lee, Michelle. "Does the United States Really Have 5 Percent of the World's Population and One Quarter of the World's Prisoners?" *Washington Post*. August 30, 2015. www.washingtonpost.com/news/fact-checker/wp/2015/04/30/does-the-united-states-really-have-five-percent-of-worlds-population-and-one-quarter-of-the-worlds-prisoners/.

Young, Peter. "The Strict Vegan Prisoner Playbook." *Vice News*. September 26, 2013. www.vice.com/read/the-strict-vegan-prisoner-playbook.

Zeveloff, Naomi. "Not Just Jews Eat Kosher in Prison." *Forward*. April 30, 2012. Accessed July 1, 2014. forward.com/news/155363/not-just-jews-eat-kosher-food-in-prison/.

# Index

# About the Author

**Erika Camplin** is a food studies scholar and has published works at *Huffington Post*, Food52.com, and other outlets.